# A Beauty That Hurts

We set out for San Mateo Ixtatán, a ride of about nine leagues....
We climbed the side of a long, high ridge, followed it and then
... came into a shaggy, rugged country of fine, tall pines and un-
canny live-oak groves, fog, cold, wheat, sheep, and very Indian-
looking Indians.... The clouds wove in and out of huge firs....
We had a glimpse of Tibet-like houses, then the clouds shut
down and the rain began.... A tall, black cross came out of
nowhere, and we began to descend. On our right, close at hand,
the other side of a new valley rose like a wall of emerald-green
pastureland seen through a shifting film of cloud.... We climbed
a hill, just enough to get back into the mist, and entered San
Mateo, getting glimpses of roses and shingle-roofed houses....
The place was mournful with rain and the constant rush of
water.... But we felt our health and spirits revive ... and all that
country was so beautiful it hurt.

– Oliver La Farge and Douglas Byers,
*The Year Bearer's People* (1931)

OTHER TITLES BY W. GEORGE LOVELL

*Conquest and Survival in Colonial Guatemala*

*Conquista y Cambio Cultural*

*"Secret Judgments of God":*
*Old World Disease in Colonial Spanish America*
(with Noble David Cook)

*Demography and Empire:*
*A Guide to the Population History of Spanish Central America*
(with Christopher H. Lutz)

# A Beauty That Hurts

## LIFE AND DEATH
## IN GUATEMALA

### W. George Lovell

For James Dunkerley ~
who's grappled with this dark
beauty, many times, himself

Abrazos,

George

BETWEEN THE LINES
TORONTO, CANADA

(Kingston, Canada ~ July 27, 1999)

Published by:
Between The Lines
720 Bathurst Street, #404
Toronto, Ontario M5S 2R4
Canada

Design: Gordon Robertson
Cover painting of San Mateo Ixtatán: Veronica Desjardins
Author photograph: Bernard Clark
Map of Guatemala, p. 2: Marcia J. Harrington
Printed in Canada

Permission to quote from the following works is acknowledged:
Rigoberta Menchú, *I, Rigoberta Menchú: An Indian Woman in Guatemala*
(London: Verso, 1984); Victor Montejo, *Testimony: Death of a Guatemalan Village* (Willimantic, CT: Curbstone Press, 1987); and Jean-Marie Simon, *Guatemala: Eternal Spring, Eternal Tyranny* (New York: W.W. Norton and Co., 1987).

Between The Lines gratefully acknowledges financial assistance from the Canada Council, the Canadian Heritage Ministry, and the Ontario Arts Council.

A contribution from Plumsock Mesoamerican Studies is gratefully acknowledged.

**Canadian Cataloguing in Publication Data**

Lovell, W. George (William George), 1951-
    A beauty that hurts

Includes bibliographical references.
ISBN 0-921284-98-5

1. Guatemala – Politics and government – 1945-1985.
2. Guatemala – Politics and government – 1985-    .
3. Human rights – Guatemala.
4. Mayas – Civil rights.
5. Mayas – Social conditions.
I. Title.

F1466.7.L68 1995    972.8105'2    C95-932232-9

Second printing, August 1996

*For my mother and my father*

# Contents

# *Preface*

THE PRIVILEGES of university life are many. One that I hold in special regard is the luxury of sabbatical leave. Released from routine and duty on my first such leave, I was able to devote myself entirely to writing, sitting at my desk without any need to prepare lectures, attend meetings, counsel students, grade papers, examine theses, evaluate grant proposals, compose letters of recommendation, or simply be at hand to help deal with all sorts of crises, real or imagined. I found peace and quiet in the woods of Vermont, where I dared to think of myself not as teacher or colleague, academic adviser or member of committee, but simply as a writer. The distinction may mean nothing to anyone else, but a Rubicon it was, and remains, for me.

My father saw things differently. When I went home for Christmas the no-nonsense ways of Glasgow were soon asserted. "Yer mother tells me yer on a year's holiday." Normally a reliable filter, on this occasion my mother had let me down badly. The words had been uttered half as statement, half as inquiry, lost on all the occupants of the Old Stag Inn but myself. I wondered, not for the first time, how to respond to my father's perception of what it is I do, what it is I am.

I began to explain, as my Dean would expect and as best I could, the gulf between "holiday" and "sabbatical," reeling off a litany of tasks I wished to accomplish before my year's leave was over. My father listened patiently. When I stopped talking it was time for another round. He wiped from his moustache the creamy froth of a fresh half-pint of Guinness. "Sounds like a holiday tae me, son!" he declared. The woman working behind the bar smiled at the sound of our laughter. Against what did my father measure his son's lucky lot? The years he spent at sea? After the merchant navy, the years spent running our family shop? After the shop closed, the years of swallowed pride sweeping the streets of Govan? As we made our way home, I felt more privileged than ever.

The flip side of privilege, however, is responsibility: responsibility to oneself, to one's family and friends, to the people and places we cherish and love, to the ideals we hope to live by. While more at ease in a university setting than in any other I have yet encountered, I have never felt comfortable with certain academic conventions. Among those that trouble me most is the bent that views scholarly work as a kind of cabal, as the ability to engage with a select group of fellow intellectuals in conversation or in print. Even if I had the inclination to express myself in such a fashion, I doubt if I would derive any pleasure from knowing that whatever I had to say could be understood, and cared about, only by a handful of like-minded specialists. The academy, at times more than I find acceptable, revels in exclusion.

So it was that, early on in my career as professor, I began to lead a double life, publishing research findings that cater to more erudite tastes while at the same time producing the odd essay or review for media with more public terms of reference. I enjoy both parts of my double life and have never considered them mutually exclusive. This book is an attempt to link and integrate the two. It is a measure of the freedom that university life allows that, during my sabbatical leave, I could channel energy into a book like this, one that draws on academic training but has non-academic goals foremost in mind. It is also, for me, a peculiar measure of what Canada represents that much of the time I spend here is taken up coming to terms with a country I stumbled on by accident over twenty years ago.

Did I choose Guatemala or did Guatemala choose me? I had been in Canada less than a year, having left Scotland to pursue graduate studies in Latin American geography at the University of Alberta. Classes in anthropology and history, to say nothing of the bite of that first Canadian winter, only fuelled my desire to flee Edmonton and head south. Responding to my supervisor's instructions—"Finish your fieldwork in Mexico and get down to Central America"—I arrived in Guatemala on June 25, 1974, not really knowing what might happen. I was twenty-three, hitching rides or travelling on second-class buses, wide-eyed and ripe for new experience. Within days Guatemala had cast its spell and seduced me completely, offering not just a fleeting summer's reward but fulfilling work for a lifetime. I had found something I longed for, something I knew would endure. I could feel it in my heart, be part of it as I walked through the hills and the corn, observe it everywhere in the bonds of land and life.

Thereafter, rites of academic passage called for a dissertation, then a monograph, with articles, conference presentations, and a teaching job along the way. Soon after being awarded my doctorate, however, I felt that something was missing, that the contract I had struck with Guatemala called for me to develop the knowledge I had picked up as a scholar, to cultivate a rapport with a more general audience. This occurred in 1981, when the political situation in Guatemala (seldom good) began to deteriorate, when friends whose safety was threatened made plans to leave, when people I knew and respected were killed. Things started to unravel, spun tragically out of control. That year I made my first foray into journalism and began to accept invitations to speak at public meetings in which issues of human rights were addressed.

Guatemala is a complex country. In trying to make sense of it, I make no claims of providing definitive, unassailable interpretations. Evidence can be presented; knowing the full extent of the truth is another matter. It will take considerably longer than has already passed for the impact of certain recent events in Guatemala to register.

The book has three parts. In Part One I let Guatemala come into focus through the lives of individuals whose circumstances differ but whose stories tell of common hardship and common adversity. These individuals also share a common will to survive, a belief that abuse and injustice can at least be confronted if not overcome. It is the strength of its human inhabitants, in particular the tenacity of its Maya peoples, that I find most fascinating about Guatemala. Part Two offers a series of temporal vignettes that deal with politics and human rights in Guatemala during the past decade and a half. For this I lean heavily for information on Guatemalan newspaper sources, because I believe that what appears each day on the printed page, however incongruous, however incomplete, is important and revealing.

In Part Three I step back from the evanescent world of journalism to assess the historical forces that shape, and the cultural context that frames, current predicaments, especially those of Maya communities. I draw here on my familiarity with archival documents and scholarly literature to inject the narrative with contemporary viewpoints and observations. I also indulge in a little playful fieldwork, which I hope lightens the load of more onerous discussion about the vicissitudes of Maya survival. Wherever possible I bring elements of the Guatemalan story back to Canada, for Canadians, as much as Americans, need to know more about life and death in a country that is closer to Toronto than Vancouver is. NAFTA has made Guatemala our next-door neighbour.

———————

As with most projects, this book reflects the help, influence, and encouragement of a number of people. A special vote of thanks belongs to Roger Bainbridge, who welcomed my very first submission on Guatemala as editor of Kingston's *Whig-Standard Magazine*. It was Roger who suggested that I start writing under a pen name, for he grasped right away the nature of my involvement, that I would always go back to Guatemala. We settled on Donald McAlpine, a combination of the maiden names of my mother and my grandmother. My *alter ego* was published in the Kingston newspaper several times. He even managed, on a couple of occasions, to migrate from the Saturday magazine to the editorial page, where his views were enshrined, if not endorsed, by the then lively, independent-minded *Whig*. In April 1982, when I testified on human rights violations in Guatemala before a parliamentary committee in Ottawa, at which representatives of the Guatemalan government were also in attendance, Donald McAlpine was made redundant. It also made sense not to return to Guatemala for a while. Roger, however, believed it his job to keep readers informed as well as entertained, as did the *Whig*'s literary editor, Larry Scanlan. From the time of McAlpine on, once or twice each year, I have written about Guatemala in the hope of making it a concrete issue, not a distant abstraction, for the Kingston community and beyond.

In addition to Roger and Larry, other *Whig* associates nudged me on at key junctures, among them Barbara Carey, Amy Friedman,

David Prosser, David Pulver, Jennie Punter, and Harvey Schachter. A colleague at Queen's University, Brian Osborne, listens with an open, supportive mind each time I return angry, sad, or confused from Guatemala. Another Queen's colleague, John Walker, insisted some time ago that I acknowledge and deal with these emotions. Numerous other university associates, at Queen's and elsewhere, I leave unnamed but appreciated. My job allows me the opportunity to talk about Guatemala in the classes I teach. Students pay me the greatest compliment when their curiosity actually takes them there, or elsewhere in Latin America.

Over the years my academic work on Guatemala has been funded by the Advisory Research Committee at Queen's University, the Killam Program of the Canada Council, and the Social Sciences and Humanities Research Council of Canada. James J. Parsons always responds in his own inimitable way. So also do Eduardo Galeano, Christopher H. Lutz, Victor Perera, and Ronald Wright. An earlier draft of this book profited from the scrutiny of Douglas Fetherling, Michael Shawcross, and Jamie Swift. Robert Clarke's talents as editor worked wonders with structure and organization. Helen Phelan and Sharon Mohammed created textual order out of handwritten chaos. Lesley and Bill Taylor encouraged an association with *The Toronto Star,* and Alastair Reid continues to be model and mentor at *The New Yorker.* Maureen McCallum Garvie has been a helpful reader and a good friend.

Words are small tokens for all that Guatemala, and Guatemalans, have given me. They are, however, the payment I am perhaps best suited to make. Words alone will never change Guatemala, but they do afford contemplation of a gnarled, captivating land, as stunning to look at as it is painful to know.

# PART ONE

*Struggle*

*and*

*Survival*

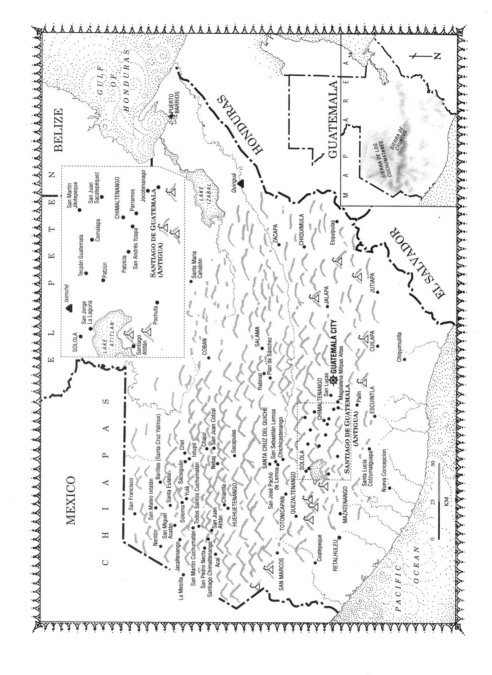

# CHAPTER ONE

# Q'anjob'al Canadian

G ONZALO MÉNDEZ was only four years old when, in 1974, I first saw the Cuchumatanes mountains that are home to him and another 150,000 Q'anjob'al Mayas. His awareness of the outside world, he told me later, was hazy, the life that awaited him in Canada unimaginable. Spanish was then as foreign a tongue as the English he now speaks fluently. His father, murdered at thirty-six, had only two more years to live.

We introduced ourselves soon after his arrival in Kingston in 1987. Gonzalo was working as a bus-boy at a restaurant, looking after tables in the summer patio. Someone at the restaurant had mentioned my name and told him about my interest in Guatemala. Gonzalo knew, for instance, that I had written a book about the experience of his people and neighbouring Mayas under Spanish colonial rule. A puzzled expression crossed his face when I said I had spent ten years researching and writing that book. He paused, then asked, "How is it possible to write a book about my people without knowing our language, without speaking Q'anjob'al?"

The question caught me off guard. I mumbled something about how "ethnohistory" and "engaged fieldwork" could elicit "the native's point of view," but I mostly felt the relevance of these notions shrivel in his stare. Whether or not Gonzalo was enlightened by my response, he didn't say. We became friends. Gonzalo moved in and shared my house with me. During our time together he told me about his long journey north, about how a Maya Indian from Guatemala came to be in Canada.

Gonzalo was born and raised in Yulá, a small Cuchumatán village of about two hundred people. Its name, in Q'anjob'al, translates as "in the water" or "in the place where there is water." Pre-Columbian in origin, Yulá today forms part of a municipal and parish division called Soloma, which is also the name of a nearby town. Soloma is itself administered as a *municipio*, or township, of the Department of Huehuetenango. The city called Huehuetenango, about sixty kilometres of bumpy road away, is an important administrative and market centre designed to serve the political and economic needs of the government of Guatemala over the entire northwestern highlands, as far as the border with adjacent Mexico. With a predominantly Ladino, Spanish-speaking population of some forty thousand, and such facilities as banks, cinemas, hotels, and video arcades, Huehuetenango is like a foreign metropolis compared to Yulá. To go from Yulá to Huehuetenango is to enter another world, to move from Indian country to Ladino city.

Gonzalo's people, the Q'anjob'al, are one of twenty different Maya groups who make up half of Guatemala's national population. Their conspicuous presence underscores a propensity for survival that few Native American peoples have been able to sustain. Maya survival hinges on how, from 1524 on, Indians in Guatemala resisted Spanish intrusion by warfare, flight, disobedience, and deception. Elsewhere in the Americas, especially in Mexico and in Peru, the lure of gold and silver guaranteed intense Spanish exploitation. Guatemala, by contrast, became something of an economic backwater, a land where Spanish conquistadors could expect only modest, marginal rewards for their adventures. In 1570, for example, a Crown official described the countryside around Yulá as "poor and unfruitful land," a place where the only commodities in abundance were "corn and chickens," hardly the stuff of which an El Dorado could be forged. Paltry resources in remote terrain often resulted in symbolic Spanish colonization, not obliterating conquest. The Q'anjob'al and other Maya peoples were thus able to create for themselves a culture of refuge that was a blend of pre-Columbian and Spanish ways, to take shelter in a culture of resistance with long-term benefits for group survival.

Far more destructive of Maya life in Guatemala than Spanish brutality or greed were outbreaks of disease. Sicknesses brought in from outside, passed from European and African carriers to vulnerable Indian hosts, served as lethal accomplices of conquest. Maya numbers dropped ninety per cent or more during the first century of Spanish rule. Population recovery was slow and sporadic for centuries thereafter.

Some years ago in a dilapidated archive in Guatemala City, I unearthed a letter about the ravages of disease among the Maya of Soloma. Dated May 5, 1806, and written by a Ladino constable named Marcos Castañeda, the letter fills me with immense sadness, for such suffering as it describes fell again on Soloma more recently, albeit for ideological rather than epidemiological reasons. The disease in question was typhus, a historic scourge of the poor. Castañeda's Bosch-like imagery and Dickensian tone of concern, the latter a rather risky attitude for a petty official to assume, evoke a grim picture of what Gonzalo's ancestors were up against. Castañeda writes:

For four years now in the parish of Soloma there has been great distress on account of the mortality caused by the typhus epidemic, which kills the Indians without relief or remedy, leaving them only in dire hardship. Through fear of death, my brother and myself fled with our families to the solitude of the mountains, suffering there from extremities of climate, leaving our houses and possessions abandoned in Soloma. But God having seen fit to end this terrible affliction, we have returned once again to our homes. We find that most Indian residents have perished and lie unburied all over the place, their decaying corpses eaten by animals which stalk the countryside.

What grieves us most, however, as it would any pious heart, is to see orphaned children crying for the laps of their parents, asking for bread without having anyone to receive it from; to behold widows and widowers mourning the loss of their consorts; and to watch old people lament the death of their offspring. After so much hard work, these unfortunate Indians have been reduced to a life of misery. Having returned from afar, those who survived are without homes to live in, for these were burned to rid them of the contagion. They are also without resources to pay their taxes and without corn to feed themselves.

If no measures are taken to assist these wretched people, they will most certainly starve to death, because they did not plant corn in the places where they sought refuge and so have nothing to live on, both this year and next, for it is now too late to plant their fields. It is a common thing in this parish to encounter Indians, old and young alike, walking from town to town, from house to house, begging or searching for corn and charity. Others seek loans, leaving as security one of their children, for they have nothing else to offer. For the sake of God and a sign of his mercy, assistance should be extended to the Indians of this parish. At the very least the people could be exempted from paying taxes for the years during which they suffered such great misfortune.

Castañeda's appeal, penned to the district governor, met with wilful disregard, a customary response. Not much changed in Soloma after Guatemala attained independence from Spain in 1821. Only in the late nineteenth century did the culture of refuge shaped by the Maya during colonial times begin to break down.

Under land and labour reforms initiated in 1871 by President Justo Rufino Barrios, Guatemala became not so much a "banana republic" as a "coffee republic." Indian lands, especially along the Pacific piedmont and in the Verapaz highlands, were taken over by enterprising coffee planters who also demanded that Indian hands be made available to perform agricultural labour. Barrios imposed on Guatemala the Liberal vision of modernity, a blueprint that would ensure plenty for a few and little for many. His double plunder, very importantly, did not affect all Maya communities to an equal extent. The integrity of some disappeared or was dissipated by the joint operation of land and labour encroachments in locales suitable for the cultivation of coffee. In other communities, including Gonzalo's, land expropriation was tempered by their being situated at elevations that were not conducive to intensive coffee growing.

The land base of Gonzalo's community may not have been usurped, but after the Barrios reforms his people began to spend part of each year working as wage labourers who migrate to Pacific plantations to help harvest coffee. Maya culture today, however, tends to be particularly resilient in communities that, like Gonzalo's, guarded their land as best they could against seizure and encroachment, even if labour was (and still is) procured for plantation deployment.

Like most Maya families, Gonzalo's has some land around which they can improvise an existence. The holder of forty *cuerdas*, about eight acres, Gonzalo's father was a wealthy man by the standards of his community. Gonzalo's family also has access to another ten *cuerdas* his mother shares with her two brothers.

Land is something Indians in Guatemala relate to in ways that transcend most Western notions of astute property management. For them land is like air and sunlight, a God-given resource over which no one exercises exclusive proprietary rights. Custom dictates that it be worked, protected, and passed on to offspring as a sacred gift handed down from the ancestors with that end in mind. Indians consider themselves not so much owners as caretakers of land.

Not surprisingly, it is in relation to land that Gonzalo's earliest memories are lodged: "I grew up on land by the side of the river. On it we raised corn, beans, chiles, tomatoes, carrots, beetroot, and potatoes. Some wheat too, higher up. For fruit we had apples, cherries, plums, and even some peaches. On our land my father kept many animals. With my sister I looked after sheep, watching out for coyotes when my father was away."

Gonzalo's father, it seems, was away quite often. The reasons for his absence were not always made clear. What Gonzalo remembers about his father comes not so much from lived experience—he was six years old when his father was murdered—as from what family and friends told him afterwards, when he was growing up.

To earn a living, Gonzalo's father worked the family land, as Indian men normally do; but he also spent time in the Ixcán, a coffee-growing region to the north of Yulá. There, unlike most other Indians, he did not pick coffee but bought it for resale elsewhere in Guatemala, primarily to merchants who shipped it overseas. Gonzalo's father was able to carve out a comfortable niche as a small-time middleman because of the capital he acquired from bootlegging, an activity that provided funds for an initial investment in the coffee business and a steady supply of cash thereafter. Bootlegging not only attracted men from all over to Gonzalo's home—men seeking refreshment or escape—but also gave his father another excuse for being on the road a lot, selling *kusha*, homemade liquor, in neighbouring villages.

In one of these villages Gonzalo's father met and formed a relationship with another woman, who gave birth in the course of the union to two daughters. Keeping a *segunda casa*, a second home, is not an uncommon practice in Guatemala. Gonzalo's father is said to have been as dependable a material provider for his "second family" as for his first.

Such situations, however, create problems. In the case of Gonzalo's father, relatives of the woman with whom he kept a *segunda casa*—her estranged husband and four drink-loving brothers—reckoned after a while that the liaison was an insult to family honour. Family honour in Guatemala is restored in several ways. One of them is murder. Whether the husband and brothers actually killed Gonzalo's father by their own hands, or arranged for others to do so, will never be known: life, we are told, is the most precious gift of all, but it can be bought inexpensively in Guatemala. Gonzalo does not rule out the possibility that his father's involvement in the *kusha* racket or his role as a coffee middleman may have been responsible for the murder. The treasury police employed by the government to track down bootleggers are notoriously vicious. Likewise, guerrillas who had infiltrated the Ixcán in the 1970s would not have considered Gonzalo's father's activities to be politically sound.

Death leaves so much unasked, so much unanswered. Gonzalo has an enduring image of his father riding off on horseback, departing on a trip. He recalls travelling with his father to Barillas once, shortly before the murder, on a coffee-buying expedition. His memories of those days are sketchy, but for Gonzalo it is important to remember his father as someone who could support his family without having to sell his labour cheaply, without having to be bossed about by others.

———

Gonzalo's sheltered life within Yulá changed when he started school. School in Yulá was then a two-room hut, attended by about thirty-five village children who were taught exclusively in Spanish by two Ladino teachers. One of the teachers also ran the local store.

Acquiring Spanish is not something all Maya children achieve with equal proficiency. Boys tend to be pushed along more forcibly during the learning process than girls, usually because they are the ones who, as grown men, will have more to account for to the Ladino, Spanish-speaking state. Gonzalo's hushed, sing-song Spanish is considerably more articulate than that of most Guatemalan Indians, many of whom command only a skeletal vocabulary of oft-repeated words, phrases, and curses. His efforts to learn and be at ease in the language of the conqueror have served him well.

Attending school brought exposure to the world beyond home and community, the world beyond the horizon. Before the trip with his father to Barillas there were shorter school outings to play soccer against the teams of surrounding villages, villages only a few hours' walk away through the fields and the forests, in valleys beyond the mountains.

Few events, however, get people moving more happily from one place to another in Guatemala than a fiesta, especially one held in association with the worship of a patron saint. Gonzalo has a warm early recollection of walking from Soloma to Santa Eulalia as part of a procession that carried a statue of San Pedro from one town to the next. Equally memorable was his first trip to the city of Huehuetenango. As a small boy he went there with his uncle to sell apples at market, and Huehuetenango remains one of his favourite places.

Maya children in Guatemala are expected to start working early. For girls this usually involves innumerable household chores: helping with babies and younger children, fetching water, washing clothes, and preparing corn to be made into *tortillas*. It may also involve learning to weave commercial items for the tourist trade. Often it means entering into domestic service in distant Ladino households, where Indian girls are rarely treated well and can be sexually harassed or even initiated while barely adolescent.

For boys priority training is coming to grips with how best to work the family plot, especially the rudiments of corn cultivation. Gonzalo was no exception. It is also common for a boy nine or ten years of age to go with his father to a plantation to be guided on how to pick coffee or cotton, shown what kind of working conditions and living arrangements to expect, and generally introduced first-hand under paternal supervision to wage employment in the Ladino world.

But when Gonzalo was introduced, soon after his tenth birthday, to the travails of plantation labour, his father was already several years dead. His initiation occurred in the company of five others from his village on a cotton plantation to the south of Retalhuleu. He lived there, along with sixty fellow workers, in a large wooden shack beside the cotton fields. Like many Indians accustomed to the cool climate of the highlands, he did not do well in the suffocating heat of the Pacific coast. He fell sick with fever and within weeks was shipped back home, where it took him months to recover.

He fared much better the next year on a coffee plantation near Santa Lucía Cotzumalguapa. There, at an altitude salubriously above the coastal plain, he worked a full forty days, earning about two dollars each day. Food and water at this plantation were less of a problem than on the cotton farm; the lodgings were cleaner and more spacious, with fewer occupants.

Gonzalo's most enjoyable and most lucrative spell as a wage labourer was on a coffee plantation, Finca La Florida, near Pochuta. He speaks almost fondly of his time there. Hard work, for sure, but good pay, tasty meals, comfortable beds, and a river nearby to bathe and even to frolic in. At Finca La Florida, in the company of his best friend, who met and later married a young woman who also worked on the plantation, Gonzalo fulfilled an eighty-day contract before returning to school in Yulá.

By age twelve he had gained enough confidence and experience to test even deeper Ladino waters. Huehuetenango, which he had visited or passed through on several occasions, would have been challenge enough. Even more so was Guatemala City.

*La capital.* Perhaps the most striking feature about Guatemala City is how it appears to bear very little relation to the land and people over which and whom it presides. If Nero fiddled as Rome burned, then the government of Guatemala is a symphony orchestra playing in the midst of even greater conflagration. What do the bright lights and commercial paraphernalia of downtown Guatemala City, the multinational consumerism and chic glitter of Sixth Avenue, the elegant mansions and flashy nightclubs of Zone Nine, have to do with the events and circumstances of a life like Gonzalo's?

I struggle with the contradictions of its capital city each time I visit Guatemala. When I mention this to Gonzalo, he shrugs. Why did he go there, what did he do there, how long did he stay there? "*Para ver.* To see what it was like. I worked as a *lustrador*, a shoeshine boy. I cleaned boots (fifty cents), and shoes (twenty-five cents) for about six weeks. During the week I looked for customers at the main bus terminal, where I'd make two to three dollars a day. On Sundays I'd go to the zoo, where I'd usually make four dollars, sometimes even five. I had a bed in a room with two other boys in a house in Zone Four. It wasn't bad."

He talks into the tape recorder so casually. It is a warm summer day in southern Ontario. The sky is blue and cloudless. Birds sing. Squirrels scramble across the lawn. The flowers gleam, the grass soaks up water, the trees provide shade. In the garden, as I listen and scribble, it crosses my mind that I first left Scotland at the same age Gonzalo left Yulá for Guatemala City. I travelled with my youth club from Glasgow to Stranraer and then across the Irish Sea to Belfast. There, playing soccer, we beat a team of boys representing a youth club on the Ormeau Road. We celebrated and slept in their church hall. We toured the premises where Cantrell and Cochrane made pop and visited Gallagher's cigarette factory. I drank free samples at the pop place, but did not have the nerve to smoke the cigarettes some of my teammates plundered at Gallagher's. I certainly would not have had the courage to head off for an unknown city and chance my hand at shining shoes.

———————

When Gonzalo returned home from Guatemala City, the countryside around Yulá had become a dangerous place to be. By 1982 insurgents who had earlier set up a base of operation in the Ixcán, the Guerrilla Army of the Poor, were at the peak of their strength. Their actions, along with those of another insurgent group, the Organization of People in Arms, were so widespread that the Guatemalan army found itself losing control over large areas of the western highlands. A desperate situation called for drastic action. It came in the form of intimidation and slaughter in rural areas where, at the local level, the guerrillas had experienced some success in building popular support for their cause.

Maya communities paid dearly for their proximity to revolution. Gonzalo's village cannot be said to have suffered the worst of counterinsurgency. Some communities no longer exist, their houses burned, their fields untended, the pens of their animals empty. The people who used to live in them are dead, scattered, or grouped in "model villages" set up by the army as a means of social control. Dreadful things happened, and much also that will never be known.

What Gonzalo knows is that guerrillas passed through Yulá late one night and painted slogans on the walls of the bridge, the church, the school, and some houses. They melted back into the darkness before dawn. The following morning the villagers awoke and looked in horror at the graffiti defacing their community.

Terrified that an army patrol might arrive and think their village a guerrilla stronghold, people set to work, daubing over propaganda with mud, paint, and whitewash. Fear lurked for days, for by then they well knew what could happen to a community suspected by the army of co-operating with the insurgents. It mattered little to the army how co-operation was gained, that it arose in many instances from the same fear of guerrillas that people have of government soldiers. Indians often could not distinguish which side was which. Whether voluntary or coerced, sympathy for the insurgent cause, however the army chose to define it, was punishable in the most barbarous ways imaginable.

Some villagers feared that the guerrillas might return first and, seeing their slogans erased, accuse people of casting their lot with the army, of being on the side of counterinsurgency. But this was deemed the lesser risk, for although the guerrillas were known to assassinate collaborators or undesirables—a woman who ran a bar in the village had been killed after she ignored warnings to stop selling liquor—their cause could never be served by indiscriminate slaughter or full-scale massacre.

The army did not itself arrive in Yulá, but an order from the regional commander did. This order called for all able-bodied men between sixteen and sixty years of age to form a civil defence patrol that would act, under army supervision, as a buffer between soldiers fighting for the government and guerrillas fighting to overthrow it.

Although civil defence patrols originated with the counterinsurgency measures of President Romeo Lucas García, it was under the rule of his successor, General Efraín Ríos Montt, that they were most actively and successfully promoted. They still exist in many areas, allegedly functioning as a means of community self-protection. Their existence is a tangible reminder not only that the threat of insurgency continues to be taken seriously, as it should, but also that it is the army, not a civilian president, that governs Guatemala.

Most Indian men resent civil defence duty. Besides forcing them to align with, and possibly even fight alongside, the national armed forces, patrol service disrupts normal working routines. It takes people away from their fields. It makes it difficult to plan projects or lengthens their time of completion. It retards mobility. It especially creates problems when a patrol member has to be absent from his community, in which case permission must be solicited, a travel permit obtained, and a suitable replacement found, persuaded, and paid to act as a substitute.

Even before Gonzalo reached the age of eligibility, he was pressed into service in the local civil defence patrol. He served as an emergency recruit, standing guard at the outskirts of Yulá while more senior patrol members were engaged in a distant reconnaissance. Not to have served, to have run away as some youths did, was to be considered subversive.

It was a scary experience. Given antiquated guns but no instructions about how to use them, one underage patrol member accidentally shot himself in the leg. Most frightening of all for Gonzalo was when he had to leave the checkpoint at the entrance to Yulá and comb surrounding hills in search of guerrillas. He had heard about exchanges of fire between insurgents and civil defence patrols in which the patrols, poorly trained and ill-equipped, had been wiped out. Although no such skirmish occurred, Gonzalo began to worry that, inevitably, one day he would qualify for regular duty in the civil defence patrol. After that loomed conscription, forced membership in an army that, as he puts it, "would teach me to hate, teach me to kill."

His fear and confusion turned to panic when, in a town called Chiquimulilla, he was apprehended by the army, thrown in jail, and interrogated. What was he doing so far from his village? Why wasn't he there serving in the civil defence patrol? Was he travelling alone or with someone else? Who did he know here in town? Where were his papers? Just awful, *muy horrible*, is how Gonzalo describes the experience of being locked up overnight, waiting for daybreak with about two hundred others in a compound that had no bunks or toilets, only enough room to stand upright.

Gonzalo had gone to Chiquimulilla with one of his relations, Cruz Sebastián, to sell ice cream at the annual fair. With earnings and some help from his mother, he and Cruz had purchased a small ice-cream maker, transported it by bus from Soloma to Chiquimulilla, found a local supply of ingredients, and set up shop. Before the army picked him up Gonzalo and Cruz had sold out their ice cream day after day. Business was terrific. He smiles as he remembers, then turns quiet and forlorn.

Luckily for Gonzalo, he was carrying a pass signed by the commissioner in charge of the civil defence patrol, which authorized him to be absent from his home for up to forty days. Cruz had taken pains to attend to this matter before he and Gonzalo had left Yulá. The pass convinced the officers who questioned Gonzalo that he was not evading service in the civil defence patrol or engaged in subversive activities in Chiquimulilla. He was later released, unharmed but shaken.

He decided to act. What he decided, at an age perhaps shy of consent but certainly not courage, meant leaving things behind: his home, his mother and sister, his friends, a land, a people, a culture. Gonzalo resolved to flee Guatemala altogether, to escape forever from the clutches of the army, first to Mexico and then to the United States.

He moved quickly. From Chiquimulilla he and Cruz travelled back to Huehuetenango. There was no time, in the rush of action, to return to Yulá and say goodbye. His mother and sister, furthermore, would try to persuade him to stay, even though they realized the inevitability of some kind of military service and Gonzalo's fears of such involvement. He asked Cruz, who was going back, to explain the situation as best he could. In Huehuetenango Gonzalo applied for papers that would enable him to enter Mexico, legally, for a short while. These he obtained without difficulty, although he lied about his age and why he wanted to leave Guatemala: he said he wanted to visit a friend in Chiapas. He sold some of his clothes, a suitcase, and the ice-cream-making equipment, not making much money. Cruz went with him to the bus station, and after purchasing a ticket Gonzalo was left with fifty *quetzales*, about twenty dollars, to his name. From Huehuetenango he travelled by bus west to the border town of La Mesilla.

The first rains had already fallen. Green with corn, the Sierra de los Cuchumatanes rose like a fortress from the banks of the Río Selegua. Gonzalo crossed into Mexico, turning his back on the past.

————

Borders are not just lines on a map. They are mental as much as geographical constructs, states of mind, not mere arrangements in space.

A border is something we carry inside ourselves, so the realms that lie on either side are in part our own creation.

Gonzalo was headed towards one of the most palpable borders in existence, the border between Mexico and the United States. Mexican writer Carlos Fuentes considers the line marked by the Río Grande less a border than a scar, a scar that divides the rich from the poor, the strong from the weak, those whom history has blessed from those whom history has damned. The scar separates not only Mexico from the United States but also the United States from all of Latin America. It is a scar that still bleeds, and the blood runs north.

Like many people from Latin America, Gonzalo first formed an image of the United States from hearsay: "I was told it was a free place, a place where there was no war, a place where you could work and study in peace. I was told that life there was easier." His perceptions were reinforced by a group of fellow Mayas he met in the Mexican city of Villahermosa. One of them, Tomás, had actually been to the United States. Like Gonzalo, Tomás and his friends had fled Guatemala—they lived in San Miguel Acatán, a town not far from Soloma—to escape the violence. Gonzalo benefited considerably from their support in Mexico. He found work as a gardener and for two months planted flowers in parks, plazas, and other public places. One of his jobs was to design the display for a floral clock. Staying in Villahermosa, however, was risky. If he was stopped by the Mexican authorities, Gonzalo was told, he would most likely be relieved of his savings and shipped off to one of the refugee camps that had sprung up in Chiapas close to the Guatemalan border. Farther north he would be safer, so with Tomás and his friends he journeyed all the way to the border city of Reynosa. There they made plans to cross the Río Grande into the United States.

Their plans worked out. Gonzalo is short in stature, but the river was low enough that one night he was able to wade across, balancing his possessions in a bag he carried on his head. No border patrol lurked on the other side. With two other Guatemalans he walked from early morning until about three in the afternoon, when they arrived at a country store. There they pooled money and called a taxi, which drove them to McAllen, Texas. Not yet fourteen, Gonzalo had made it to *El Norte*.

His good luck continued. Tomás, who had crossed the border a few days earlier, put his wits to good use. First, a place to stay. Next, a job to pay the rent. Gonzalo found work on a farm between McAllen and Edinburg. He fed chickens some of the time, fed fighting cocks the rest. Weeks passed uneventfully, and then his luck ran out.

Outside a store in Edinburg, where he had gone to buy bread and milk, officers from the U.S. border patrol questioned him politely, but insistently. Unable to produce papers, Gonzalo simply informed them he was Mexican. The officers escorted him by car to the border and watched as he walked across the bridge back into Mexico.

Deportation was only a momentary setback, for it was clear to Gonzalo that what he had done once he could easily do again. Early next morning, near Hidalgo, he waded once more across the Río Grande. His second stint in Texas, where he watered orange groves near Edinburg, lasted about a month before *la migra*, the U.S. Immigration Services, caught up with him. Gonzalo again declared he was Mexican, and he was again delivered back to Reynosa. This time he stayed longer, thinking things over. The trick, it seemed, was not just to cross the border but to get far enough inland to a bigger place than either McAllen or Edinburg, to a place where the work of *la migra* might be less efficient. He looked at a map and opted for Houston.

He waded once again across the Río Grande. After drying off in Texas he made his way to the Greyhound station in Edinburg, where he caught a bus that sped up Highway 281. He had gone about seventy miles inland to Falfurrias when a border patrol flagged down the bus. An officer boarded, approached Gonzalo, and asked him his nationality. This time he told the truth: "*Guatemalteco*." Guatemalan, not Mexican. The officer did not believe him. Gonzalo was ordered off the bus and put in a waiting patrol car. He was taken to headquarters in Falfurrias where, when questioned, he repeated he was Guatemalan. His truthfulness was finally taken seriously. Instead of being accompanied back to the border, Gonzalo was driven to a detention camp for Central American aliens located halfway between Brownsville and Harlingen, near a place called Los Fresnos.

For an entire month Gonzalo fretted in detention. During this time he was noticed by a visitor to the Los Fresnos camp, his youthful Maya features standing out among the older, predominantly *mes-*

*tizo* (mixed Spanish-Indian) traits of other Latin detainees. The visitor contacted a local church group that had decided to challenge U.S. immigration law by offering sanctuary to individuals and families, especially from Central America, who had fled their homes through fear only to be denied refugee status in the United States. Through the mediation of the sanctuary movement, Gonzalo was released from detention; a bond was posted with U.S. Immigration Services to guarantee future knowledge of his whereabouts. He was taken to Baton Rouge, Louisiana, where he was placed in the care of Quakers, who welcomed him as one of their own.

Gonzalo lived with the Quakers for three years. In Baton Rouge he began adjusting to life in El Norte. Different sights, different sounds. Different wants, different needs. A different sense of time, a different sense of place. Different premises to wake up to in the morning, different expectations to go to bed with at night. It was all, he says, just so vastly different, especially the language. Learning English was not easy, but immersion in school and at home—he spent hours and hours in front of the television—soon produced encouraging results. Today, Gonzalo's spoken English is impressive, softly voiced and less noticeably accented than that of most Latin American immigrants.

He had two options concerning how to secure the legal right to remain in the United States. The first was to apply for status as a resident alien, a costly, protracted procedure, one that might not produce the desired outcome. The second was to be adopted officially as a member of the family he was living with in Baton Rouge. Of the two options the second carried the best chance of success, but it necessitated formal severance of ties with his natural mother—and acknowledgement of this step on her part as well as his.

The paperwork for option two was pursued, but Gonzalo could not bring himself to follow it through. It represented an emotional barrier far more difficult to traverse than trekking through Mexico and crossing the Río Grande. Moreover, he worried that his legal adoption in the United States would get his mother into difficulties, for word had reached him that she had been questioned about his absence from Yulá.

As the dilemma grew, another option materialized. A church organization in Georgia found out about Gonzalo's case and suggested that permission to enter and reside in Canada might be more readily attained than applying for resident alien status in the United States. Contact was made with a refugee support group in Kingston, whose members were informed of the particulars of his situation. Despite changes to Canadian immigration law, an application to allow him to enter Canada as a landed immigrant was processed favourably in six months. Judging from the dozens of cases I've been consulted on since, I reckon that getting his immigration papers in prompt, satisfactory order was a stroke of considerable luck.

Gonzalo took leave of the Quaker family in Baton Rouge. He did not want to go, but neither did he wish to squander an opportunity to enter another country on a firm legal footing. He boarded a plane and arrived in Toronto several hours later. At age seventeen, four years after he fled Guatemala, Gonzalo's life as a Q'anjob'al Canadian had begun.

# CHAPTER TWO

# Nobel K'iche'

R IGOBERTA MENCHÚ spoke in Toronto the day *The Globe and Mail* ran a travel feature with the headline "GUATE- MALA IN STYLE FOR A MERE $5 A DAY." I have no idea whether she or the organizers of the human rights conference she came to address noticed the piece. I suspect, however, that the image of Guatemala it projected would not have been to her liking.

It is unclear from the piece whether or not the writer, Margaret Piton, had actually visited Guatemala: she provides the prospective tourist with a long list of enticements, but these are mostly culled from Paul Glassman's *Guatemala Guide*. Piton packages Guatemala as cheap, romantic, and not to be missed by anyone interested in an exotic travel experience. She writes:

> The ideal travel destination would probably be a country with beautiful scenery, a spring-like climate, nice beaches, historic buildings and ruins, fine handicrafts, and low prices. Such a country does exist—and it isn't on the other side of the world. Guatemala has all the above attributes and can be easily reached in a day's travel.

Piton goes on at length about the glories of Guatemala. Then, towards the end of her piece, she offers the following reflection:

> There is no such thing as a perfect travel destination and Guate- mala, like every country, has problems. Poverty is widespread and petty theft is common in some areas—especially markets.

Political violence flares up from time to time, although the situation seems to have improved with the present civilian government.

The Guatemala that Rigoberta Menchú speaks of is far removed from the "low prices," "beautiful beaches," and "tasty, filling meals" that Margaret Piton writes about. Menchú's message to the people gathered in Toronto's Church of the Holy Trinity—that we live in a careless world, one that acts wantonly and forgets too easily—could not have been more timely.

Menchú recounts the details of her life in Guatemala in a compelling oral history given shape, structure, and the authority of print by Elisabeth Burgos-Debray, a Venezuelan scholar who pieced together, in autobiographical form, interviews she conducted with Menchú in Paris in 1982. After the publication of her testimony in Spanish in 1983—an English translation *I, Rigoberta Menchú: An Indian Woman in Guatemala* appeared a year later—Menchú began to travel across Europe and North America speaking about her beloved but tormented Guatemala. Her work as a human rights activist was instrumental in her being awarded the 1992 Nobel Peace Prize.

A Guatemalan Indian of K'iche' Maya lineage, Menchú was twenty-three years old when she and Burgos-Debray recorded her testimony. Burgos-Debray recalls:

> Rigoberta spent a week in Paris. In order to make things easier and to make the best possible use of her time, she came to stay with me. Every day for a week, we began to record her story at nine in the morning, broke for lunch about one, and then continued until six in the evening. We often worked after dinner too, either making more recordings or preparing questions for the next day. At the end of the week I had twenty-four hours of conversation on tape.

The transition from spoken to written word, Burgos-Debray informs us, involved two key stages:

> I began by transcribing all the tapes. By that I mean that nothing was left out, not a word, even if it was used incorrectly or was later changed. I altered neither the style nor the sentence struc-

ture. The Spanish original covers almost five hundred pages of typescript.

Burgos-Debray then set about the tricky job of editing Menchú's words in order to lend them narrative coherence:

> I soon reached the decision to give the manuscript the form of a monologue: that was how it came back to me as I re-read it. I therefore decided to delete all my questions. By doing so I became what I really was: Rigoberta's listener. I allowed her to speak and then became her instrument, her double. . . . This decision made my task more difficult, as I had to insert linking passages if the manuscript was to read like a monologue, like one continuous narrative. I then divided it into chapters organized around the themes I had already identified. I followed my original chronological outline, even though our conversations had not done so, so as to make the text more accessible to the reader.

The text created by Burgos-Debray, like that of most oral histories, is not without problems. Menchú is at times repetitious, obscure, vague, and inconsistent. She collapses separate episodes into a single event, mixing time and place in ways that would incense academic purists, especially those who believe in the myth of objective social science. Collective memory is of necessity selective memory, subjective memory. Such ways of remembering are simply how the K'iche' and other oral cultures operate. They are also, in large measure, the reason why Menchú's testimony has such universal appeal. the voice that working with Burgos-Debray has given her speaks as much for an entire people as for one person. Her experiences in Guatemala also form the centrepiece of a documentary film, *When the Mountains Tremble* (1983). Soon after her week in Paris with Burgos-Debray, long before the heady days of the Nobel laureate, Menchú became an important cultural icon.

This unusual status for an Indian woman is linked directly to the power of her testimony. Menchú begins by telling about her father, mother, and brothers and sisters, and about growing up not just in the remote highland village where she was born but also on plantations on the Pacific coast where her family, like most Indian families, spent part of each year picking coffee or cotton. The trip from the *altiplano*, or highlands, down to the plantations, known in Guatemala as *fincas*, is not one for a delicate stomach:

> I remember the journey by lorry very well. . . . The lorry holds
> about forty people. But in with the people, go the animals (dogs,
> cats, chickens) which the people from the *altiplano* take with
> them while they are in the *finca*. . . . It sometimes took two
> nights and a day from my village to the coast. During the trip the
> animals and the small children used to dirty the lorry and you'd
> get people vomiting and wetting themselves. . . . The lorry is
> covered with a tarpaulin so you can't see the countryside you're
> passing through. . . . The stuffiness inside the lorry with the
> cover on, and the smell of urine and vomit, make you want to
> be sick yourself just from being in there. By the time we got to
> the *finca*, we were totally stupefied; we were like chickens coming
> out of a pot.

Years spent working on *fincas*, where one of her brothers died from
pesticide poisoning and another from malnutrition, were followed
by a spell serving as a maid in a well-to-do household in Guatemala
City. Menchú's memory of domestic service abounds in details of
abuse and degradation:

> The food they gave me was a few beans with some very hard *tor-
> tillas*. There was a dog in the house, a pretty, white, fat dog.
> When I saw the maid bring out the dog's food—bits of meat,
> rice, things that the family ate—and they gave me a few beans
> and hard *tortillas*, that hurt me very much. The dog had a good
> meal and I didn't deserve as good a meal as the dog.

Washing dishes and mopping floors, however, was not without
reward, for it was in such exploited keep that Menchú groped
towards a knowledge of Spanish.

Learning Spanish changed her life. Following the example of her
father, a community activist, in 1977 Menchú joined a peasant organization responsible for raising the political consciousness of rural
workers. Being bilingual meant that as well as working in her own
and other K'iche'-speaking communities, she could travel throughout Guatemala and communicate with Ladinos, Spanish-speaking

persons of mixed European and Maya descent who, in her words, "also live in terrible conditions, the same as we [Indians] do." By the late 1970s, as civil war between guerrillas and the national armed forces began to take a heavy toll, Menchú aligned herself firmly on the side of the insurgents, committed to revolution as the only means of achieving peasant demands for human rights and social justice.

Counterinsurgency war has scarred Rigoberta Menchú's life, like that of many Guatemalans, in horrible ways. She tells how, on September 23, 1979, in the company of her parents and fellow villagers, she watched Guatemalan soldiers burn alive her sixteen-year-old brother and several others accused of co-operating with the guerrillas:

> The lorry with the tortured came in. They started to take them out one by one.... Each of the tortured had different wounds... but my mother recognized her son, my little brother, among them.... My brother was very badly tortured, he could hardly stand up.... He was cut in various places. His head was shaved and slashed. He had no nails. He had no soles to his feet. The earlier wounds were suppurating from infection.... I found it impossible to concentrate, seeing that this could be. You could only think that these were human beings and what pain those bodies had felt to arrive at that unrecognizable state.... My mother wept. She almost risked her own life by going to embrace my brother. My other brothers and my father held her back so she wouldn't endanger herself.... The captain said, "This isn't the last of their punishments, there's another one yet...." They lined up the tortured and poured petrol on them; and then the soldiers set fire to each one of them.

Four months after this incident Menchú's father was also burned alive. He was killed in a blaze that gutted the Spanish Embassy in Guatemala City when it was fired at by government security forces ordered to end a peaceful occupation by Indian leaders protesting against repression in the countryside. Then, in April 1980, her mother was kidnapped, beaten, and raped, left to die after being dumped by the army on a deserted hillside far from the Menchú family home:

When my mother died, the soldiers stood over her and urinated in her mouth; even after she was dead! Then they left a permanent sentry there to guard her body so that no-one could take it away, not even what was left of it. The soldiers were there right by her body, and they could smell my mother when she started to smell very strongly. They were there right by her; they ate near her, and, if the animals will excuse me, I believe not even animals act like that, like those savages in the army. After that, my mother was eaten by animals; by dogs, by all the *zopilotes* [vultures].

Menchú writes that the soldiers stayed at the site for four months, "until they saw that not a bit of my mother was left, not even her bones, and then they went away."

As a text, one that has been read in translation in over a dozen languages, Menchú's testimony has had an immense impact. How she comes across in print, however, does not compare with the experience of hearing her in person. When she spoke that evening in Toronto, dressed in a colourful, wraparound skirt and a sleeveless Indian *huipil* that defied the February cold, she was sitting around a table among fellow Guatemalan exiles, joking as well as consoling, laughing one minute, sombre the next. As I listened to the way she kept her family alive by telling vivid details of their deaths, I was struck more than ever by the enormity of Maya survival, by the courage of her people in suffering, enduring, and coming through. That vital human trait is what she manifests in remarkable personal fashion and communicates to her listeners.

Two years after hearing her speak in Toronto I was asked to translate for Menchú while she was doing a speaking engagement in Kingston. Moves to nominate her for the Nobel Peace Prize had just begun. It was a gala community event, complete with a potluck supper, attendance by the mayor, and a book-signing turned into a marathon by her earnest desire to inscribe each copy of her text with the best wishes of the author. It was nearly eight o'clock when the audience settled down to hear her speak.

The church hall had few empty seats. We sat side by side on the stage. "*Me llama Rigoberta Menchú y este es mi testimonio. . . .* My name is Rigoberta Menchú and this is my testimony." Her voice was calm but plaintive, her words measured, sure, precise. She spoke for almost three hours, which exhausted me more than it did her. Then she fielded questions. It was well after eleven when the evening ended.

After the audience had dispersed, Rigoberta thanked me for my services and apologized for the number of instances she had spoken beyond the length of time suitable for ideal translation. She then said something that will stay with me always.

"You understand, Jorge," she whispered, "that I can't tell them everything I know, everything that happened. If I do that, they might not believe me. I can only tell so much. It's better that way."

# CHAPTER THREE

# Through the Eyes of Jean-Marie

I MAGINE, if you can, the naked body of a young woman. Her head is turned to one side, eyes closed, lips apart, mouth half-open. She is dead. A soiled cloth has been laid across her genitals. Her arms, in repose, are arranged across her chest, but they have no hands. These, apparently, have been cut off, one placed beneath her right arm, another on top of her stomach. The left side of her face shows she was pretty, but the right side has been mutilated. Three deep gashes on her right arm stand out amidst myriad other lacerations. She must have departed life, had it taken from her, in a frenzy of agony. An ooze of yellow matter, uncontained by stitches sewn from skin to skin by the mortician, runs along what was once the top of her breasts. The polish with which she painted her toenails somehow withstood the torture inflicted on her, for the nail of her big toe, left foot, has a fleck of red unmistakably lighter in colour than her dry, crusted blood.

Her name is Eugenia Beatriz Barrios Marroquín. Like Guatemala itself, this image of one of its citizens, one of its victims, screams in silence, a tragedy we glimpse through the steely eyes of Jean-Marie Simon. Simon came across the corpse in the town morgue at Escuintla. It is important for Canadians to know something about the particulars of this case, for Beatriz Barrios had solicited, and received, formal permission to enter Canada as a political refugee. She had been issued a visa and was abducted only a day or so before she was due to leave Guatemala for Canada. In *Guatemala: Eternal Spring, Eternal Tyranny* (1987), Simon writes:

On December 10, 1985, two days after [Vinicio] Cerezo's presidential victory, 26-year-old Eugenia Beatriz Barrios Marroquín, a school teacher and mother to two small children, called for a taxi to go to a friend's home.

Minutes after she left in the taxi, she and the driver were stopped by a car carrying three armed men, who forced her out of the taxi and into their vehicle. Barrios had either been under heavy surveillance or the call that she made to the taxi dispatcher had been monitored by government intelligence. Although the taxi driver returned to tell her friend about the abduction, it was too late.

Her body was found the following day, near Palín, Escuintla, by the painted quetzal-bird rock: it had been hacked, her face carved out, her hands severed at the wrists. A piece of cardboard found near the body carried her name and the words "more to come." When security agents arrived to take fingerprints from her severed hands, Captain Armando Villegas, head of the Honor Guard G-2 intelligence office, was already there. When they asked him, "Muchá, what happened?" Villegas responded by taking out a card on which he had written Barrios's name, and told them that it was she. The writing on Villegas's card matched that on the cardboard message.

In her book Simon documents the sweep of events that, between 1982 and 1987, saw Guatemala pass through "two presidential elections, two military coups, two states of alert, two Constitutions, an eleven-month state of siege, at least four amnesty periods, and four heads of state—three of them army generals." Today, even though a civilian president ostensibly governs, the army continues to exercise tremendous clout. Nowhere is this more apparent than in the so-called "Ixil triangle" of the Sierra de los Cuchumatanes, a militarized zone whose fields, folklore, people, and communities are highlighted throughout Simon's riveting photo-essay.

It was in Ixil country, at the Pensión Tres Hermanas in Nebaj, that I last spoke with Jean-Marie Simon. I'd noticed her from afar earlier in the day, walking across the town square in quick, determined bursts. I had some sad news to tell her, of the death of a dear friend of mine, someone she also knew, who in fact had introduced us years before at a bookstore in Antigua. I figured I'd bump into

her later on, for Nebaj is that kind of place. We ended up eating supper together in the kitchen of the *pensión*. Conversation was hushed,
for the facilities at Tres Hermanas attracted soldiers from the army
barracks only blocks away, who rented rooms for their trysts with
visiting prostitutes.

Jean-Marie was careful not to tell me too much about what she
was doing in Nebaj, but she was there to say goodbye. The country
she first visited in 1980 had consumed her talents for the better part of
a decade. A gutsy, driven individual, willing to confront face-to-face
the unpredictable horror that death in Guatemala can look like, Jean-
Marie had taken risks in getting her photographs that not many would
be prepared to incur. It was time to move on—marriage and a law degree were on the horizon—before Guatemala claimed any more.

We said goodnight. I found myself thinking: What, as a photo-
journalist, does Jean-Marie Simon leave behind as a record of her
years in Guatemala?

As a photographer she has an eclectic range. Her touch is varied,
her vision confident and keen. She moves skilfully from dark to
light, capturing in the mood of her pictures the chameleon landscape with which she wrestles—tender, cruel, cathartic, bleak, a pattern with no fixed design. She is careful to make us celebrate as well
as mourn. Her photographs demand that we rejoice, not just
lament, for "a nation of prisoners" is also "a nation of survivors."

As a journalist, a consultant to Americas Watch and Amnesty
International, she focused on contemporary issues of human rights.
The flagrant, incessant, and bestial violation of human rights in
Guatemala had in Jean-Marie Simon a dogged reporter. The text of
her book is informative, but her photographs are what set her apart.
They are indeed striking, and they form an impressive collection.
An Ixil mother, child in her arms, circled by government soldiers,
stares towards us during interrogation. Stopped at a roadblock, a
passenger on board a bus peers from the window. Dawn at Nebaj,
the white walls of the church rising above the mist that shrouds
rooftops and cornfields. A member of the armed forces dances with
a young girl at a party, a machine gun slung across his back.

Think about what you see, her images beseech, when you look
at the world. Let your gaze not be idle. Through the eyes of Jean-
Marie, Guatemala soothes and disturbs, nurtures and kills.

# CHAPTER FOUR

# Arbenz and the Fruit Company

THE STORY of Jacobo Arbenz and the United Fruit Company could easily be mistaken for an artful invention by Graham Greene or John Le Carré. Political sabotage is the name of the game, in which an elected government not to the liking of the United States is destabilized and removed from office by covert action code-named Operation Success.

The liberator, handpicked for his anti-communist convictions, is a corrupt lackey later gunned down in the presidential palace by one of his own bodyguards. Other protagonists include a gun-loving U.S. ambassador and a diplomat who, though his country's highest representative in a Central American state, speaks no Spanish. The plot involves psychological as well as physical warfare and is peppered with campaigns of misinformation, bribes, payoffs, arms shipments, secret memos, and the recruitment of foreign mercenaries.

There are even two bizarre suicides: one is the twenty-five-year-old daughter of the deposed president, who shoots herself in a crowded restaurant after quarrelling with her boyfriend, a bullfighter; the second is a shady, deranged businessman, who throws himself from his office window, forty-four floors up, to the oblivion of the street below. The ousted president, an idealist who sought only to give his impoverished people a better lot, himself dies mysteriously in exile, drowning in a bathtub in Mexico. Such characters and scenarios, alas, spring not from the world of fiction but from the sad annals of Guatemalan history.

In 1944, popular unrest and a revolt by junior officers in the armed forces led to the overthrow of President Jorge Ubico, a strong-arm general who had ruled Guatemala for fourteen years. Elections held the following year saw Juan José Arévalo, a schoolteacher, sweep into power with more than 85 per cent of the vote. During his six-year term of office, from March 1945 until March 1951, Arévalo was guided by concerns for agrarian reform, protection of labour, a better educational system, and consolidation of Guatemala's fragile political democracy. Commitment to the last goal in particular called for repeated vigilance, but having survived numerous plots by dissident right-wing factions to dislodge him, Arévalo, after another election in November 1950, was able to hand over the presidency to Jacobo Arbenz Guzmán, a captain in the armed forces who assumed office by gaining some 65 per cent of the votes cast.

Central to Arbenz's designs for a new Guatemala was an agrarian reform that sought to redress chronic landholding disparities and the appalling social and economic inequalities that accompany them. In 1950 agricultural workers could expect to earn an annual income of around $87. According to a census taken that same year, 2.2 per cent of the nation's landowners managed 70 per cent of Guatemala's total arable land. Of about four million acres in the hands of plantation owners, less than one-quarter was actually under cultivation at any given time. U.S. corporations invested heavily in Guatemalan agribusiness, to the tune of some $120 million. The largest and most powerful U.S. corporation was the United Fruit Company, known in Guatemala either as *la Frutera* ("the Fruit Company") or, perhaps more revealingly, *el Pulpo* ("the Octopus").

In June 1952 the Guatemalan Congress approved legislation devised to empower the Arbenz government to expropriate uncultivated portions of large plantations and turn them over to landless peasants. The value of expropriated land was related directly to its declared taxable worth, a provision that enraged certain targets, particularly United Fruit, since for years its property had been deliberately undervalued in order to reduce tax liability. During the following eighteen months, some hundred thousand poor Guatemalan families received a total of 1.5 million acres of formerly uncultivated land, for which the reform authorities paid $8.3 million in government bonds. Arbenz expropriated about 400,000 acres of land from United Fruit, offering in return $1.25 million, a figure based entirely on the company's own taxation records.

United Fruit's response constitutes one of the most repugnant acts in Latin American history. Manipulating its close connections in Washington, United Fruit was able to convince the White House that a "Red Menace" in Guatemala threatened U.S. business and security interests. It then wooed the Central Intelligence Agency into masterminding, at an estimated cost to U.S. taxpayers of $20 million, the overthrow of the Arbenz government, ushering into power a repressive *junta* headed by Colonel Carlos Castillo Armas, whose forces, protected by U.S. air strikes, invaded from neighbouring Honduras. Betty Jane Peurifoy, the wife of the U.S. ambassador to Guatemala, immortalized the moment in lines later published in *Time* magazine:

> Sing a song of *quetzals*,
> Pockets full of peace!
> The *junta*'s in the Palace,
> They've taken out a lease.
> The Commies are in hiding,
> Just across the street;
> To the embassy of Mexico
> They beat a quick retreat.
> And pistol-packing Peurifoy
> Looks mighty optimistic
> For the land of Guatemala
> Is no longer Communistic!

The only air strikes Arbenz could launch were on the radio. On the second day of the invasion he declared:

> Our only crime consisted of decreeing our own laws and applying them to all without exception. Our crime is having enacted an agrarian reform which affected the interests of the United Fruit Company. . . . Our crime is our patriotic wish to advance, to progress, to win economic independence to match our political independence. We are condemned because we have given our peasant population land and rights.

In his final broadcast Arbenz spoke with valedictory bluntness:

> For fifteen days a cruel war against Guatemala has been under-
> way. The United Fruit Company, in collaboration with the
> governing circles of the United States, is responsible for what is
> happening to us. . . . In whose name have they carried out these
> barbaric acts? What is their banner? We know very well. They
> have used the pretext of anti-communism. The truth is very dif-
> ferent. The truth is to be found in the financial interests of the
> fruit company and the other U.S. monopolies which have
> invested great amounts of money in Latin America and fear that
> the example of Guatemala would be followed by other Latin
> countries.

Although United Fruit has long since departed, the legacy that it
and its supporters imposed on Guatemala lives on, inflicting on the
hearts and minds of thousands of people wounds that can never heal.
If the United States had allowed Arbenz to govern without intervention, if the democratic process he was part of had been encouraged rather than violated, the carnage of the 1980s might have been
averted. I have been haunted by this thought ever since a senior
member of the Reagan administration lamented the impossibility of
getting hard-liners in Guatemala to co-operate, declaring thirty
years too late, "Oh, for an Arbenz now!"

A seed, once tended, bears fruit. People must eat it, if given
nothing else, in order to survive. The after-taste lingers. And poi-
sons still.

# CHAPTER FIVE

# Witness to Slaughter

J ACALTENANGO is a remote, unkempt-looking town at the western edge of the Cuchumatanes mountains close to the Guatemalan border with Mexico. It is best known to the scholarly world as a stop on the route taken in 1925 by Frans Blom and Oliver La Farge, who afterwards produced a two-volume memoir, *Tribes and Temples* (1926, 1927), about their reconnaissance. La Farge returned to Jacaltenango two years later with fellow researcher Douglas Byers, with whom he penned *The Year Bearer's People* (1931), another classic, pioneering contribution in the field of Mesoamerican anthropology.

Both works, but especially the latter, document an intriguing array of Maya survivals. One of the most remarkable was the persistence in Jacaltenango of a method of observing the passage of time according to a pre-Columbian calendar, complete with rites and ceremonies that date back centuries if not millennia. In his introductory remarks to *The Year Bearer's People*, Blom aptly likened the intent of La Farge and Byers "to that of a man trying to become familiar with the ritual of a Masonic Lodge without becoming a Mason himself." All three men spent long and distinguished careers studying indigenous cultures in Guatemala and other parts of the Americas.

More recently Jacaltenango has captured the attention not of visiting anthropologists but of one of its native sons. Victor Montejo has given local lore and storytelling eloquent written form in two books, *El Kanil: Man of Lightning* (1984) and *The Bird Who Cleans the World* (1991). The first book presents an elaborate legend that La Farge and Byers recorded only fragments of; the second is a collection of fables that resonate with the moral authority of Aesop. In *Testimony* (1987), however, social not magical realism prevails as Montejo grapples with his own and his people's lot during counterinsurgency operations in Jacaltenango in 1982.

On the morning of September 9 that year, a Friday, Montejo woke in a small village some distance from Jacaltenango. During the week he taught classes as the resident master in the village school. Friday, he tells us, "has always been a happy day for me, full of anticipation," for after class he would set off to return home to Jacaltenango to spend the weekend with his wife and children. A primary schoolmaster, Montejo had worked for ten years as a government employee in the Department of Education, preferring to take a humble post within reach of his home rather than teach in a more illustrious setting further away. Montejo was satisfied with his decision to go back to his roots after graduating from teachers college.

That Friday class unfolded as usual until one of the villagers burst into the schoolhouse and screamed, "The guerrillas are approaching. . . . Everyone get ready!" The peal of the church bell confirmed the danger. Montejo recalls:

> I consulted my watch and saw it was eleven in the morning. At almost the same instant I heard the first shot fired. Behind it came a volley of machine gun fire. The peaceful community broke into confusion. The women wept and prayed to God to protect their husbands and older sons who had been forced to join the civil patrol.
>
> I ordered the students to stretch out on the floor and barred the door and windows with old broomsticks. The invaders had encircled the village and the hills echoed the furious explosions of grenades and the sputter of bullets that whistled past the corrugated tin roof of the schoolhouse.
>
> "Don't make a sound," I ordered my children. Some began to weep and others trembled with fear. Their fathers were in the midst of that gunfire, armed with sticks, stones, and slingshots and the children were fully aware of the danger they were in.

It turned out to be a tragic case of mistaken identity. The local civil patrol had seen an armed group of men moving through village territory and assumed they were guerrillas. The patrol opened fire, wounding one of the intruders, but then noticed that the guns the intruders replied with were emitting the distinctive "coughing noise of Galil rifles," the standard Israeli-made issue of the Guatemalan army. Realizing their error, the members of the civil patrol fled to escape retaliation.

Chaos erupted as the army attacked the village. After a while the shooting died down, and Montejo felt it was safe enough to dismiss his students, who "fled like deer out the door" and raced off to find their parents. He then joined other villagers ordered by the army to assemble in the school patio. There and in the space adjoining the village church the army was getting ready for a public execution, rounding up local militiamen who had been captured and accused of being guerrillas. They tied five men to a row of pillars. Montejo attempted to intervene and explain to the enraged officer in charge just what had happened:

"Good afternoon, my lieutenant," I said respectfully. . . .

"What do you want, you—" he snapped.

"I am the schoolmaster in this village and have come to let you know that the people you're holding captive are members of the civil patrol. By accident they mistook you for guerrillas."

"Don't come to me with those stories. These sons of bitches are guerrillas. That's why they attacked us, and I am going to execute every damn one of them."

I went on, unperturbed. "Up there by the chapel the rest of the men are waiting to clear up the situation for you."

"With me you have nothing to clear up. Everything is already clear. They've wounded one of my soldiers, and all of you will have to pay for it. What more do you want to know?"

"I beseech my lieutenant to forgive these people. All the men are members of the patrol and guard the village day and night, as you have verified for yourself. What a pity they mistook you, because of your olive green uniforms."

The commander made no reply, but went on inspecting [some] boxes and chests. . . . "This radio interests me. Take it along," he called out.

Montejo's intervention proved futile. The lean majesty of his prose only heightens the horror of what took place next, when the firing squad did its work:

The five condemned men turned to one another, uncomprehending. They set their eyes above the heads of the *kaibiles* [soldiers] who were lining up to discharge their weapons into their hearts. No one spoke. The hapless captives gazed toward the horizon, as though to bid farewell to the hills that had nurtured them. . . .

As the commander prepared to give the fatal order, the condemned turned instinctively for a last look at their loved ones. Their hands were tied behind their backs so they could give vent to their feelings only with strained smiles and bitter tears.

"FIRE. . . !" The cavernous voice of the commander rang out, and the Galils exploded with thunderous fury.

The women raised a deafening howl. Dazed with grief, they tried to fling themselves on the bullet-ridden bodies of their beloved ones, but once again the *kaibiles* forced them to draw back by threatening them point blank.

The victims slumped and hung from the pillars as the warm, copious blood drenched their shirts.

After the execution Montejo's personal situation quickly deteriorated. Under torture a villager demented by pain gave Montejo's name as a guerrilla sympathizer, and so the schoolmaster was sought out, bound, beaten, and led "like a thief or a murderer" back to army headquarters in Jacaltenango, where he was interrogated and beaten again. Death, he believed, seemed inevitable:

I was bothered by the knotted rope around my neck and stuck my fingers repeatedly under the noose to prevent it from choking me. My dignity as a schoolmaster, I said to myself. These bastards are making a display of me, as if I were an assassin, a thief or a common criminal. I spat my darkest unspoken thoughts on the ground. . . . In all my thirty years I had not known darker days than the present ones.

Fortune, however, favoured him. Insisting always on his innocence, Montejo was eventually released from captivity, but only on the condition that he visit army headquarters and report on "every person" he thought might be "involved with the guerrillas." Repugnant though this condition was to him, he accepted it to protect himself and his family. Once home, living by his wits for weeks on end, he resisted being forced to inform on others until he was finally able to flee into exile and arrange for his wife and children to follow. The family now lives in California, where Montejo teaches anthropology. After he departed Guatemala suspicion fell on his parents, and they also fled. They now live in Ottawa.

In recording his ordeal Montejo is careful not to lapse into indiscriminate hatred. During his captivity a soldier offered him food and a blanket, and Montejo reflects: "I thanked God that not every soldier was malevolent and devoid of human feelings. His gesture made me understand that in their own way—although they dare not say so—they too are victims of a violence that has become institutionalized." The crude Spanish spoken by most of the soldiers involved in the operation allowed Montejo to identify them as natives of Sololá or Totonicapán, Mayas like himself.

With a heavy heart Montejo observes how terror sows division and distrust among Maya communities, how it corrodes group solidarity. The scorn with which the soldiers rebuked his pleas of reason—"you don't fool any of us with your high-sounding jabber"—illustrates how risky it is to value education in a country in which knowledge or the gift of self-expression can be construed as subversive.

Now, instead of instructing school children in Guatemala, Montejo finds himself lecturing to university students in the United States. He has adjusted to the demands of this new challenge with customary Maya resourcefulness, working hard in graduate school to earn both a master's degree and a doctorate. I enjoy bumping into him at conferences, where he is a vocal critic not only of human rights abuses in Guatemala but also of the failings of modern anthropology, which Montejo says too often portrays Maya culture as static and residual, not vibrant and alive. He counts La Farge and Byers among his most esteemed and abiding influences and recently translated *The Year Bearer's People* from English into Spanish. While he appreciates the benefits of a settled life outside Guatemala, his heart still lies in Jacaltenango.

Death or exile has been the fate of many Guatemalan intellectuals. Having dodged death, Montejo lives out his exile wondering when, if ever, he will be able to return home safely.

# CHAPTER SIX

# Doña Margarita

W E ARRIVED in Santa Cruz del Quiché shortly before noon, drove slowly around the main square, then waited as instructed in front of the church. I spotted Tina before Lorenzo did. She made her way unhurriedly across the plaza, looking relaxed and composed. I found it remarkable to think that she had given birth to a baby girl only days before. Everything with Tina was the opposite of drama. She specialized in being matter of fact, which made her a reliable stringer.

I heard her call out our names as she approached the jeep. We nodded. "You're early," Tina said. "Doña Margarita's eating lunch. The women from CONAVIGUA have still to arrive. You can order something to eat also before we head out to San José." Lorenzo's contacts had come through. We might yet get the film footage he wanted.

Margarita Hernández, eighty-five years of age, polished off her soup but picked rather than ate her way through the main course. She complained about the *tortillas*, which looked and tasted like burnt cardboard. She drank her Pepsi *al tiempo*, unchilled, straight out of the bottle. Flies buzzed around the table. Doña Margarita declined coffee but accepted the offer of tea. She had the most weathered face I have ever seen, rutted with deep lines that absorbed shiny beads of perspiration. Her grey hair was braided in pigtails tied with strands of bright pink ribbon. We sat in the restaurant waiting for Josefa and Tomasa. The bus from Guatemala City, naturally, was late.

When the women from CONAVIGUA arrived they too had to eat. While their meals were being prepared they brought Doña Margarita into the conversation, which our lack of K'iche' and her limited Spanish had hitherto prevented. All three Maya women chatted away in their native tongue, with Josefa and Tomasa translating into Spanish for our benefit, as well as relaying questions into K'iche' for Doña Margarita to answer. Doña Margarita was clearly at ease with the two much younger women, who had helped her with her earlier petitions. The time we spent together in the restaurant set things up nicely for the on-camera sequences Lorenzo was to shoot in San José.

There was room in the jeep for one passenger only. Tomasa volunteered. Josefa rode with Doña Margarita in Tina's car, along with Tina's baby girl and her nanny. We followed them for about half an hour along the dusty, dry-season road. Boys and men were hard at work readying the fields before the onset of rain. Tomasa explained to us her and Josefa's involvement in CONAVIGUA, the widow's support group Doña Margarita had contacted in her efforts to recover the bodies of her husband and her son.

San José Pachó de Lemoa is a hamlet of some twenty to thirty houses near the larger settlement of San Sebastián Lemoa, to which it owes administrative allegiance and social affiliation. Doña Margarita was born in San Sebastián and lived there until she married at age twenty. Her husband, one year younger than her, persuaded her to move to San José because his family compound offered more space and better access to land. Doña Margarita's mother had died years before, and her father died soon after her marriage, so she convinced her husband that his orphaned in-laws, three girls and two boys, should move also to San José. The eldest of seven—one of her brothers died early on, after becoming sick while working on a coffee plantation—Doña Margarita kept an eye out for her siblings while raising a family of her own, a son and two daughters. She and her husband worked hard. He tilled their land and sought contracts as a hired hand. What he loved most was to play the *marimba*. He was also an accomplished drummer, which made him an important member of the village band. Doña Margarita is good with her hands too. Since age seven she has woven *trenzas*, narrow palm bands used to line the inside of hats. She rarely sits at home without the trappings of her craft scattered around her.

The family compound in San José is home to over fifteen people, from toddlers to the elderly. Doña Margarita's daughter-in-law lives there, with her children. A grandson, fifteen years of age and Doña Margarita's favourite, was only an infant when his father was murdered. He never really knew what his father looked like: all he has to go on is his parents' wedding photo, which shows bride and groom looking stiff and uncomfortable in clothes that don't seem to fit. Doña Margarita's grandson says he looks at the photograph, pinned to a wall alongside a religious calendar and a poster of the Brazilian World Cup soccer squad, every day.

Lorenzo flutters from one side of the compound to another, worse than the resident chickens. "I'm worried about the light," he says for the umpteenth time. "Two things. Ask the old lady if she can turn around a bit so her face is in the sun. And could she stop weaving hat bands? The rustling noise her hands make interferes with the sound of her voice. It'll muddy up the tape." It is Tomasa's turn to be go-between. Doña Margarita lays down her *trenza* at the same time Lorenzo lays down his camera. She reaches for the soft drink Tina brought her, sipping through a straw from a plastic bag while Lorenzo loads a new battery. "Right. Ask her when she's speaking not to look at the camera," he says to Tomasa. "Tell her to look over my shoulder." Doña Margarita starts to talk again, in accordance with Lorenzo's wishes.

She speaks mostly about her son. A member of the local co-operative and a church group called Catholic Action, he laboured for the betterment not just of his family but also for the community as a whole. It was Doña Margarita's son who lobbied to have San José connected by a dirt road to the main highway. He was the one who hounded the authorities in Santa Cruz del Quiché to install running water and build a school. He knew how to read and write and wanted others to learn too. After the earthquake in 1976, when the church was levelled and had to be rebuilt, he organized the people who did the work. All these initiatives made him well known, distinguished him from the crowd. He was liked by most but not by all, for there were some in the community who thought him aloof, arrogant, smart, and pushy, too big for his boots. "People who get things done make people who do nothing jealous. Jealousy breeds hatred. That's how it is." Doña Margarita's words ring true for more than just the small-town ways of San José.

Whenever she warned him about people talking about him, Doña Margarita's son shrugged it off. "I do what I think needs to be done," he would say. Even he, however, admitted that it was best to maintain a low profile when the situation deteriorated in the early 1980s, for Doña Margarita's son was precisely the kind of individual whose social awareness was considered a threat, whose "Catholic Action" was interpreted as "communist subversion." When the worst of the killings were under way, he cooled his heels and even took leave of San José for a while. His absence, however, only fuelled the local rumour mill and served to increase suspicion on the part of his enemies that he was up to something.

The date is etched forever in Doña Margarita's mind. She mouths it with the reverence of prayer: *"Era la tarde del día domingo veintiseis de diciembre milnovicientos ochenta y dos. . . .* It was the afternoon of Sunday, December 26, 1982." She and her husband were at home when members of the civil defence patrol arrived, entered the family compound, and demanded to know the whereabouts of their son. Her husband answered that their son had gone off to work in Guatemala City. The patrol members accused Doña Margarita's husband of lying. They threatened him in an attempt to get him to disclose the truth. He insisted that he was telling them the truth, but still they would not believe him. When he resisted attempts to be bound and taken captive, he was punched and kicked. Then an old man in his seventies, Doña Margarita's husband was soon overpowered. He was led away with his hands tied behind his back, shoved and cursed. He has not been seen since.

After the abduction of her husband, Doña Margarita chose the same manner of dealing with the tragedy as countless thousands of Guatemalans: silence. Through fear of reprisal from denouncing the crime, she sought instead to cover it up. What she feared most was that her son would hear of his father's disappearance and return to San José.

How word reached her son she doesn't know, but his response to the news, as expected, was to go home to see his mother. Doña Margarita again has no difficulty remembering the date: February 12, 1983. The *orejas*—the Spanish name for "ears," meaning spies or informants—did their job with numbing efficiency. Soon after Doña Margarita's son entered the family compound the civil defence patrol also arrived. He was surrounded, tied, beaten, then led under armed guard to the schoolhouse, where he was detained. Doña Margarita followed all the way to the schoolyard, weeping and pleading. Members of the patrol threatened to kill her unless she left immediately. *"Escuché un disparo. . . .* I heard a gun go off and knew it was him, that my son was dead."

At this point in her story she pauses to wipe her eyes. Tomasa translates in a voice that becomes so quiet it is barely audible. Josefa takes over as Doña Margarita resumes.

For almost ten years it was deemed unsafe and unwise to bring the matter to anyone's attention. Then a fear stronger than reprisal began to eat away at Doña Margarita: that she herself would die without giving her son a proper burial. Maya Catholicism can be an unorthodox, hybrid faith, but it is practised at all times by people who believe that the dead must be buried with dignity and respect. Doña Margarita got in touch with CONAVIGUA through her church. CONAVIGUA, in turn, engaged the interest of the forensic scientist Clyde Snow, whose research team took the case on as part of an attempt to come to terms with Guatemala's unwholesome past.

People in San José knew where to look. At the bottom of a ravine not far from Doña Margarita's home only a thin layer of soil covered her son and five other victims. She watched with her grandson and daughter-in-law as the bones were unearthed. A dozen or so locals also looked on. Exhumation allowed positive identification and the opportunity to allay grief with decent burial. The remains of Doña Margarita's son now rest in peace. The remains of her husband have yet to be found.

*"Es raro,"* her grandson says. "It's strange. We know who killed my father. They are our neighbours. One lives right over there and two others just up here." He gestures with his arms this way and that, aware that his grandmother is listening.

"When we meet them out walking, we still say hello," he says. "We talk with them, but not about my father. He's never mentioned. We talk about other things: animals, the price of food, how the corn is doing. They know we know. But we don't do anything. I don't know why."

Doña Margarita sighs, then picks up her *trenza* and starts to weave.

PART TWO

*Blood*

*and*

*Ink*

# CHAPTER SEVEN

# The Delivery Man

J OSELINO arrives with the newspapers every morning shortly after seven. He prefers to ring the doorbell rather than summon attention with the brass knocker cast in the shape of a hand. When I open the door I usually find him flicking through the pages, stealing a glance at the headlines between call and answer. His bicycle is propped against the curb on the side where the foot pedal is missing, an entire day's delivery stacked in the wooden box fitted above his rear wheel. After work Joselino rides a flashy motor bike, as impressive to behold in the streets of Antigua as his handsome, kiss-them-and-leave-them looks. He peers up at me from beneath the peak of his baseball cap and grins. His dark eyes sparkle, but it's the gleam from the gold in his teeth that dazzles most. "*Buenos días,* Jorge!" he declares, even though the news he delivers makes for anything but a good morning.

Knowing that I live in Canada, Joselino informs me that there's nothing about it mentioned in today's papers. I recall once reading about "Brain" Mulroney attending a G-7 summit meeting, and the sports section occasionally announces the scores and standings of the Blue Jays and the Expos. But not much news about Canada filters south to Guatemala.

One morning Joselino asked if Canadian papers carry news about Guatemala. Not very often, I told him. I also told him that, as part of my job, I write from time to time about Guatemala, but that the content and style of my efforts are usually quite different than the standard fare of the Guatemalan press. With a cry of "*Hasta mañana!*" he jumped back on his bicycle and resumed his round.

I thought afterwards about Joselino's question and the kind of news that daily fills the delivery box on his bicycle. I also thought about the dozens of times I get asked, "How was Guatemala?" on my return to Canada. I clip bits and pieces from the newspapers that Joselino delivers each time I visit Guatemala, and afterwards I file them with my field notes as a record of the trip. Those yellowed clippings and scribbled notes allow me to look back and remember.

# CHAPTER EIGHT

# Into the Fire
# (1981)

T HE MAN sitting next to me in the sauna is a doctor from Guatemala City. He has come out to Jocotenango in the hope that he can cleanse himself of more than just the capital's filth. The story he tells me concerns one of his colleagues, Raúl Matamoros, also a doctor. They had grown up together, gone through medical school together, worked at the same hospital together, and were the best of friends.

"I said good-night to him on Thursday around six. Next morning, when he didn't show up for his shift, people asked me if I knew where he was. I told them I'd no idea, that he'd left to go home when I did. Later on Friday his secretary called me and told me they'd found his body. Two bullets, one on each side of the head. And knife wounds too."

A woman on the other side of the metal partition shouts, *"Más leña, por favor."* I hear a door creak open and a man curse as he stokes the fire. The doctor shakes his head.

"I'll never understand it," he says. "He lived properly and correctly. He cared for people. He loved to read and was good at his job."

The lumps of wood thrown in below us start to crackle. The metal partition ticks.

"We buried him yesterday," the doctor continues. "He was my age, thirty-two, with a wife and two little girls."

I ask the doctor if he knew of a reason. Another shake of the head.

*"Listo para su masaje!"* I hear a voice holler. Yes, I'm ready for a massage. I excuse myself with a quiet *"Con permiso."* The blood of one doctor is the sweat and tears of another.

That night I catch up on a backlog of newspapers. An article in *El Gráfico* of May 31 suggests that the killing was *"una equivocación,"* a mistake, but reveals that Raúl Matamoros was a prominent figure in soliciting relief funds for the needy after the earthquake of February 4, 1976.

If Guatemala can ill afford the loss of a caring doctor, so too the life of a rural schoolteacher. A June edition of *El Imparcial* reports:

### Teacher Gunned Down
### in Front of 40 School Children

A primary school teacher was shot to death by unknown assassins in the village of Sanjón, in the Department of San Marcos, in full view of forty of his pupils, according to local authorities.

The victim was identified as Adolfo Recinos Ramos, thirty-seven years of age, who was shot a number of times, dying instantly at the scene of the attack.

Recinos, moments before, had left the small country schoolhouse of Sanjón and was walking to the bus that would have taken him to his home in nearby Malacatán.

With him walked some forty of his pupils, who were accompanying Ramos to the bus stop. Two unknown men suddenly blocked his way and opened fire.

The body of the murdered schoolteacher was taken to the morgue of San Marcos national hospital at 8:30 p.m. yesterday, three hours after the shooting.

Teachers, it seems, are prime targets for "unknown assassins." The headline in *El Gráfico* on June 4 announces: "Five Teachers Gunned Down: One in San Lucas, Three in Nueva Concepción, and One More in the Capital." Particularly hard hit is the University of San Carlos, one of the oldest universities in the Americas, now a skeleton of learning: scores of its professors and students have been murdered or intimidated into silence, while others have sought refuge outside the country. Some have taken to the hills to join the guerrilla insurgency. On June 25, celebrated throughout Guatemala as Teachers Day, leaflet bombs that exploded in a number of cities declared the founding of the Frente Revolucionario de Maestros, the Revolutionary Teachers Front.

Not all teachers targeted for death meet their end quickly. Some mysteriously "disappear," only to show up dead a week, a month, a year later. In the June 3 edition of *El Gráfico* we learn:

### Kidnapped Teacher Found Dead

The schoolteacher Bertha Alicia Morán González, twenty-three years of age, who was abducted on Saturday, May 23, was found dead in the early hours of the morning at 14th Avenue and 8th Street in Zone 6 of Guatemala City.

Beside the teacher's body there was also the corpse of a forty-year-old man, as yet unidentified. The family of the deceased teacher visited the morgue at San Vicente hospital, where they identified her body.

The teacher had been abducted on May 23 after leaving her home to attend a birthday party to be held in her honour at a neighbour's house.

Her body was found with the same clothes she had on at the time of her abduction.

In this case the report mentions no evidence of rape or torture, but sexual assault and disfigurement often await the victim between disappearance and death. Another account, from the *Prensa Libre* of May 25, records the murder of journalist Fulvio Alirio Mejía, who worked for the newspaper *La Nación*. Journalism, like teaching, can easily be interpreted as "subversive" and is therefore a profession that is practised under censure of death. Alirio Mejía's death is again but one example of many:

### Journalist Was Disfigured
### Bodies of Other Persons
### Also Found Butchered

The body of the journalist Fulvio Alirio Mejía, which mysteriously appeared in Cuilapa, Santa Rosa, along with the bodies of various others, showed signs of cruel torture, attributed primarily to blows from a *machete*.

His face was a mass of deep wounds, apparently perpetrated to produce chronic disfigurement and thus prevent recognition of his body. He was also stripped of his clothes, but his wife, Esmeralda Chavarría de Mejía, was eventually able to identify him.

He and the people found with him had received the same treatment as persons now turning up dead all over Guatemala. Badly beaten and amputated bodies have appeared in many localities. All of them show signs of torture, some the ominous mark of strangulation.

The naked or semi-clad bodies of the five people found with the corpse of Alirio Mejía included a nine-year-old boy and other juveniles, all of whom were brutally disfigured. The murder of all six victims was an abominable act, especially the butchering of the nine-year-old who, in addition to being knifed in the face, also had his tongue cut out. When reporters arrived in Cuilapa seeking information, the grave diggers had begun to bury the five juvenile bodies. Because no family members were there to identify them, they were laid to rest in an unmarked common grave. Several locals offered prayers to the Almighty for the eternal rest of their souls.

Alirio Mejía "reappeared" and, despite the mutilated condition of his corpse, was identified by his wife. The sorrow of relatives and friends of other victims who vanish but do *not* reappear is prolonged indefinitely. Such is the case of the journalist Rodrigo Ramírez Morales. According to a July 16 report in *El Gráfico*, Ramírez had still not "reappeared" following his abduction, one month earlier, by a group of armed men. He had been driving his car one day in June, accompanied by his wife. She, like many others, placed a notice in the newspapers beseeching his captors to spare his life and to allow him to return home, in this case to five children. The pleas of distraught next-of-kin, which appear with photos of disappeared loved ones in the personal columns, not too far from notices of bereavement, make unpleasant reading. The following is no exception:

DISAPPEARED: The family of Licenciado Oswaldo René Cifuentes de León once again appeals, in the name of God, to those who have it in their power to release him. Already his

absence has brought much pain and suffering to his home, especially to his mother Marta de Cifuentes and to his wife Elvia de
Cifuentes, who are in great distress at not knowing his whereabouts. His infant son cries to have his father back with him.
The family begs those who hold him to respect his person and to
let him return home, for he is a man dedicated to his family and
to his profession. He has never been involved in any kind of
political activity. At the same time his family begs the Supreme
Creator that those responsible for his captivity never have to suffer what they are going through now, but that He forgives them
and makes them see the error of their ways. Any information
will be gratefully appreciated. God will pay you back.

Into such cases few official inquiries are made. Seldom is anyone
brought to trial. This is hardly surprising, for while a criminal element undoubtedly exploits the situation, most acts of violence can
be attributed to the government itself. If the government were to
pursue the cause of justice, its own soldiers and police officers would
be the ones brought before the courts.

This is not to deny that acts of violence are also perpetrated by
guerrilla insurgents. The guerrillas, however, tend to strike swiftly—
at army convoys, at retired or off-duty soldiers and policemen. The
work of the death squads, by contrast, is often sadistically deliberate—designed, so it seems, to inflict maximum physical suffering on
the victim and maximum psychological anguish on the next-of-kin.

At times, though, the national armed forces move into action
with Draconian speed. This was apparent on July 9 and 10 when, on
two separate occasions, guerrilla "safehouses" in different neighbourhoods of Guatemala City were located, surrounded, and attacked, resulting in over thirty deaths. Perhaps the most harrowing
aspect of these two episodes is that when the bodies of the deceased,
including eight women, were displayed in La Verbena morgue, a
number of them—judging, said *El Gráfico* of July 12, from the reaction of people looking for missing relatives—were obviously recognized and could therefore have been identified. But because people
feared that reprisals would accompany any known association with
the dead, no-one spoke up. The corpses were interred, marked with
an anonymous double X, in yet another common grave.

The heavy-handedness of these two operations (artillery and

tanks were brought in) is somewhat unusual, for they occurred in fairly well-to-do neighbourhoods of Guatemala City, in Colonia El Carmen and in Vista Hermosa. The countryside, not the capital city, is more commonly the location of the heaviest fighting, particularly the departments of Huehuetenango and El Quiché. So great is the strife in these two departments—remote, mountainous, the ideal terrain in which to wage a guerrilla war—that the government is careful not to allow news of all that happens there to reach the press. Such is the case with events that took place in early June in the town of San Mateo Ixtatán, a community of Chuj-speaking Mayas in the northern reaches of Huehuetenango.

On June 4 the front page of *El Gráfico* showed two young Indian boys in the local hospital. The caption beneath their photos reads:

> Juan Domingo Martín is one of four survivors of the actions of a heavily armed group of men who invaded the homes of the townspeople of San Mateo Ixtatán, murdering thirty-six men, women, and children. The young boy does not speak Spanish and has no serious injuries, but is now an orphan, for his mother and father were killed. The other young boy, named Andrés Gómez Diego, gravely wounded, tries to tell reporters, in poor Spanish, some of his impressions of what took place.

At this point the newspaper story fizzles out. Perhaps the editor of *El Gráfico* considered it unwise to print the information he received. He may even have been advised *not* to print it. What I heard was that the guerrillas, as they do often, took over San Mateo briefly at dusk. Speaking to residents in *lengua*, the native tongue, they held a meeting and explained their goals and motives in an attempt to win local sympathy and support. After the speechmaking was over, the guerrillas withdrew to the safety of the hills. Night fell and the townspeople went to bed.

Alerted to the presence of guerrillas, by what means were never made clear, the army arrived shortly after midnight. Their search proved fruitless. Frustrated, the soldiers turned on the townspeople themselves, but not before they had been ordered by their commanding officer to take off their uniforms and put on civilian clothes.

Massacres like the one at San Mateo are calculated to frighten survivors into shunning all contact with the guerrilla insurgency, which the government chooses to view as an external, not domestic, reaction to decades of neglect and exploitation. Vinicio Cerezo Arévalo, the leader of the Christian Democracy Party, puts it succinctly: "My government would have you believe that communism is the enemy of democracy in Guatemala, when in reality the government itself is freedom's greatest foe."

Meanwhile, in an attempt to improve its image at home and abroad, the government of General Romeo Lucas García has launched a propaganda campaign. It portrays itself as pushing ahead on all social fronts—health, education, land reform, housing, installation of water and electricity, and the creation of new jobs. Along the Pan-American Highway, carved into thick walls of volcanic ash, above fresh asphalt and a widened surface, a message declares: IN PUBLIC WORKS LIKE THIS THE GOVERNMENT OF GENERAL LUCAS INVESTS YOUR TAXES. Ironically, but not surprisingly, the tourists expected to make use of the improved highway system grow fewer and fewer. A hard-hitting editorial in *El Gráfico* addresses the related issues of political violence, foreign image, and the collapse of the tourist industry:

### Guatemala, A Tourist Paradise
### —But Without Any Tourists

The hotel business in this country, upon which the livelihoods of thousands of Guatemalans depend, is in a state of crisis, a crisis brought on by the understandable decline of foreign tourism, principally from North America and Europe. This decline affects not only the hotel business but also many other related activities, such as tours organized by travel agencies and the handicraft industry, which are directly linked to the inflow of visitors.

In Quezaltenango, a recent convention had as its main focus the hard times that have fallen on hoteliers not just in the capital but throughout the country, on account of the drastic decrease in tourism, which has already forced the closure of one important hotel, the Cortijo de las Flores in Sacatepéquez, and threatens the closure of others. Guatemala is an open book of Latin American history: the richness of our pre-Columbian and colonial heritage is well recognized, set in landscapes of dream-like beauty and in one of the most agreeable climates in the world. All this means nothing, however, when viewed alongside the violence that afflicts our country today. This image, projected abroad, is the main reason behind the decline in tourism, a business that thrived here not long ago.

Conservative estimates place the drop in foreign visitors over the past year at twenty per cent. But we believe this figure to be an optimistic one. We must confront the reality of our situation and not bury our heads in the sand.

What is said about Guatemala in other countries exerts a powerful influence over the well-being of tourism. Violence prevails in our country today, violence we see escalating each day in the number of kidnappings, murders, and attempts on human life. A recent bulletin released by Associated Press lists Guatemala, along with El Salvador, as being among parts of the planet currently in a state of war. Violence is something that has spilled beyond our borders to the notice of the outside world, and this is something we cannot hide. The decline of tourism is damaging, particularly because its vibrancy over the past few years assisted our economy and helped us withstand the effects of the collapse of coffee on the international market. Until a short time ago, Guatemala showed to the rest of humankind a friendly, cheerful face. Today we are a sad and preoccupied people. And the splendour of our landscapes, the kindliness of our weather, the richness of our culture can do nothing to change that demeanour.

Like most foreigners who visit Guatemala, I have fond memories of time spent there. The temples of Tikal under a full solstice moon. Walking the streets of Antigua at dusk. Jacarandas and flame trees. The blaze of bougainvillaea on an old church wall. Early morning sounds at Lake Atitlán. Mist in a cornfield at dawn. The smell of burning *pom* at Chichicastenango. Cutting open a *pitaya*. Smiles and grins on market day. Driving through the countryside, offering people lifts, then listening to their stories. After rain, watching the sky clear and the light fall on Volcán Agua.

To the voice inside that asks, "How can you marvel at beauty in the midst of so much pain?" I have yet to find an answer.

# CHAPTER NINE

# Peace of the Dead
# (1982–83)

I MISSED THE VISIT of Pope John Paul II by only a few days. He was in Guatemala on March 7, 1983, during one of his whirl-wind pastoral engagements. Part of his address to an assembly of Maya Indians was delivered in K'iche'. "The Church is aware of the discrimination you suffer and the injustices you must put up with," the Pope told his audience. "It raises its voice in condemnation when your dignity as human beings and children of God is violated."

Pope John Paul's words were spoken exactly one year after General Angel Aníbal Guevara was said to have won an election even the most blinkered of Guatemalans knew to be rigged. Discontent with the election outcome so troubled junior officers in the armed forces that they closed ranks and plotted a coup that led to the overthrow, on March 23, 1982, of the government headed by General Romeo Lucas García. The removal of Lucas García brought about the political resurrection of the man denied the presidency in the fraudulent elections of 1974, General Efraín Ríos Montt.

From their days in military college the junior officers responsible for the coup remembered Ríos Montt as a soldier of impeccable integrity, an honest, moral, consummate professional. They asked him to head a military *junta* that also included General Horacio Maldonado Schaad and Colonel Francisco Luis Gordillo.

Ríos Montt re-entered national politics at a time of widespread public disgust with the Lucas García administration. There was also growing concern among the armed forces that the war against guerrilla insurgents was not yielding satisfactory results. Ríos Montt, it was hoped, would turn things around. Three stages can be distinguished that allow an assessment to be made of the consequences of the junior officers' coup, consequences that can be attributed in large measure to the return of Ríos Montt.

---

Stage one lasted a little over five months, from March through August 1982. It represented, in essence, the declaration of war on any individual or group suspected of assisting, or even sympathizing with, the guerrilla insurgency. This phase of counterinsurgency was especially harmful to Maya communities within whose territory the Guerrilla Army of the Poor and the Organization of People in Arms had established a strategic, insurgent base. Having realized, to paraphrase Mao Tse Tung, that the Indians were the water in which the fish to be caught swam freely, the armed forces unleashed a fearful repression on native peoples—worse than anything experienced under Lucas García, whose soldiers were responsible for an estimated 27,000 killings between 1978 and 1982.

One of the first public notices of renewed and even intensified atrocities came on May 12, 1982. Following a peaceful occupation of the Brazilian Embassy in Guatemala City, members of a peasant organization known as the Committee for Campesino Unity (CUC) issued a statement later circulated among the national and international press. The CUC declared:

> We wish to denounce before our people and the peoples of the world the brutal repression that the Indian communities of Guatemala are suffering at the hands of the military *junta*'s army. We wish it to be known that this *junta* of generals and colonels, since March 23, has not only continued the policy of massacres and destruction practised by the previous military government, but in some regions has intensified the massacres to levels never before experienced. Since March 23, far from seeing an end to the massacres, we have seen the *junta* continue and intensify the massacres.

The CUC's claim was reiterated, only five days later, in an editorial that appeared in *El Gráfico*. Signed by the newspaper's general director, Jorge Carpio Nicolle, the editorial observed:

Massacres have become commonplace, massacres in which no respect or mercy is shown for grandparents, children, or grandchildren. Shortly before the coup we published an editorial entitled "At least spare our children." The cases discussed in that article are very similar to the current one: excessive use of force, unrestrained sadism, psychotic mercilessness. It would be difficult for any person in their right mind to imagine this kind of extermination. How is it possible to decapitate an eight- or nine-year-old child? How is it possible for a human adult to murder, in cold blood, a baby of less than a year-and-a-half? In war, one cannot hope for mercy on the field of battle. That is understandable, but not the actions of someone who kills defenceless non-combatants, children and old people who are not involved in anything. Nor is it acceptable to murder pregnant women, for these acts of bestiality only serve to sink the nation deeper into the most degenerate immorality.

On May 20, 1982, another editorial ran:

To anyone who has any sympathy with their fellow human beings, the kind of genocidal annihilation taking place in the Indian areas of the country is truly horrific. There has been much talk of improving our image abroad, but this image will continue to darken more and more with this new resurgence of blind and absurd violence. This new resurgence of mass murders sends the message that Guatemala is very far from peace, or even experiencing a decrease in violence. The outside world will once again close its doors to us, because in fact we do not deserve any kind of foreign assistance as long as these episodes continue.

The *junta* headed by Ríos Montt denounced such allegations as a smear campaign organized by the international Marxist press, pointing to a fall in the body count in major towns and cities as evidence of its good intentions. Shortly thereafter the *junta* attempted to improve its image by offering, from June 1 on, an amnesty to all those who had fought against it. The guerrillas ignored the amnesty. On June 9 General Maldonado and Colonel Gordillo were removed from their posts as members of the *junta*, leaving Ríos Montt to be named President of the Republic.

One of Ríos Montt's first acts as president was to impose press censorship, a measure taken "to avoid publications that spread confusion, cause panic, or aggravate the situation." He also decreed, effective July 1, a state of siege, which allowed secret tribunals to operate—tribunals invested with the power to impose the death penalty. Declaring a state of siege in effect allowed the government to legalize repression and to grant security forces an even freer hand in their operations.

Throughout the month of July the slaughter of Maya Indians continued. In one incident involving the remote community of San Francisco, near Nentón in the Department of Huehuetenango, the army entered the village, gutted houses, burned crops, slayed livestock, and killed over three hundred men, women, and children. One eyewitness, whose account was corroborated by fellow survivors who fled to Mexico, recalls the scene:

> The soldiers took our wives out of the church in groups of ten of twenty. Then twelve or so soldiers went into our houses to rape our wives. When they were finished raping them, they shot our wives and burned the houses down.
>
> All our children had been left locked up in the church. They were crying, our poor children were screaming. They were calling us. Some of the older ones were aware that their mothers were being killed and were shouting and calling out to us.
>
> They took the children outside. The soldiers killed them with knife stabs. We could see them. They killed them in the house in front of the church. They yanked them by the hair and stabbed them in the bellies; then they disembowelled our poor little children. Still they cried. When they finished disembowelling them, they threw them into the house and then brought out more.
>
> Then they started with the old people.
>
> "What fault is it of ours," the old people said.
>
> "OUTSIDE!" a soldier said. They took the poor old people

out and stabbed them as if they were animals. It made the soldiers laugh. Poor old people, they were crying and suffering. They killed them with dull *machetes*. They took them outside and put them on top of a board; then they started to hack at them with a rusty *machete*. It was pitiful how they broke the poor old people's necks.

They began to take out the adults, the grown men of working age. They took us out in groups of ten. Soldiers were standing there waiting to throw the prisoners down in the patio of the courthouse. Then they shot them. When they finished shooting, they piled them up and other soldiers came and carried the bodies into the church.

A survivor of an earlier massacre, who also fled to Mexico from neighbouring Huehuetenango, depicted the desperate plight of his people in a painting with the caption: "This is the village of Acal, where the army massacred the people on Wednesday, May 26, 1982, when they were all in church. When they realized what was happening the soldiers had already surrounded the village. That is why we see many people dead and hanging and lying on the ground." According to Amnesty International, between March and July of 1982 over two thousand Indians were slaughtered in sixty separate acts of violence. The Mexican Christian movement Justice and Peace suggests that the human toll was considerably higher: nine thousand killings in the five months following the coup.

In an attempt to escape the carnage, thousands of Maya families abandoned their communities. They sought refuge in the mountains, in the squatter settlements of Guatemala City, in the plantations of the Pacific coast, and in refugee camps across the border in the Mexican state of Chiapas. Even to people for whom conquest and subjugation have been a way of life for centuries, Ríos Montt's first five months in office rank among the bloodiest of times the Maya have known.

———

A second stage of counterinsurgency lasted from September through December 1982. These four months saw a reversal of tactics, best described as a shift from physical to psychological war.

Having terrorized rural communities and prompted the retreat of an estimated four thousand guerrilla combatants, the armed forces scaled down their search-and-destroy missions, replacing them with a program called the Plan of Assistance to Areas of Conflict, better known as *frijoles y fusiles*, "beans and rifles." Aware that its scorched-earth forays had created a large number of hungry as well as dead Indians, the army demanded that in return for the provision of food, towns and villages set up civil defence patrols to keep future guerrilla encroachment at bay.

The message was clear: comply and be fed, equivocate and be killed. Since it was by now evident that the guerrillas were no match for the army, that alliance with the insurgents (real or perceived) spelled death and destruction, Maya communities across the highlands realized the imperative of co-operating with their aggressors. By year's end hundreds of towns and villages had formed civil defence patrols in which local residents, under army directives, maintained guard against guerrilla penetration.

Ríos Montt claimed personal responsibility for the success of the "beans and rifles" campaign. Speaking in Honduras during President Reagan's visit to Central America in December 1982, the general explained:

> In response to subversive activity we have developed a combined security and development program known as our "beans and rifles" policy, to provide for the needs of the peasant farmers in the war zone. Farmers who have been prevented by threat of terrorist attacks from working their fields are being furnished with food by the government, and in return they provide the labour to repair the physical devastation caused by the terrorists. At the same time, the very real threat they now face from the terrorists has not been overlooked. We have granted the farmers the right to defend themselves militarily. In 850 largely isolated and previously helpless villages, 300,000 Indians have now been organized into civilian self-defence units which, armed with home-made rifles, patrol their towns and fields and can fend off terrorist attacks when necessary.
>
> The overall success of the program has been striking. Vast areas have been recovered from terrorist control, allowing local officials to be reinstated. We have reopened schools and health

centres. Social service teams travelling in the wake of the army have provided food, shelter, work, and medical attention to Indian peasants left destitute by the strife around them.

The general also claimed responsibility for a twelve-point code of conduct supposed to govern the behaviour of his troops when they dealt with civilians, especially in rural areas. The code stated:

1. I will not take so much as a pin from the villagers.
2. I will not make romantic overtures towards the women of the district, nor take advantage of them.
3. I will protect and take care not to harm the crops growing in the fields through which we travel.
4. I will pay a fair price for what I buy. In case of doubt, I will offer to pay more.
5. I will return anything I borrow and pay for anything that is damaged.
6. I will be courteous, treating the elderly and children with special affection and respect.
7. I will receive anyone who wishes to speak to me pleasantly and courteously.
8. I will respect the customs and traditions of the villagers, and be respectful also of their civilian and religious authorities.
9. On the highways and roads I will yield the right-of-way any time this does not jeopardize the security of the troops.
10. I will not accept gifts or exaggerated compliments from the rich or powerful.
11. I will not take unfair advantage of the inhabitants' hospitality in the countryside.
12. I will observe respect for graves, sepulchres, churches, and other structures that are respected by the community.

Like Spanish conquistadors, whose actions centuries earlier were also cloaked in high-sounding rhetoric, Ríos Montt's soldiers conformed to only one code of conduct: *"Obedezco, pero no cumplo. . . . I obey, but I do not act accordingly."*

Stage three of Ríos Montt's offensive began in December 1982 and was still under way when I was in Guatemala during the months of February and March 1983. Known as *techo, trabajo y tortilla*—shelter, work, and food—this stage was alluded to by the general when he addressed President Reagan in Honduras, informing him: "The underlying philosophy of 'beans and rifles' is that permanent security ultimately comes only through economic development, social justice, and progress. Thus the initiative known as 'beans and rifles' will gradually be expanded into an ambitious and comprehensive development program to improve the *campesino*'s life permanently." President Reagan was said to be impressed.

A striking characteristic of Ríos Montt's strategy of food for allegiance was that many of the groups sanctioned by the government to organize community development were Protestant evangelical sects based in the United States. Ríos Montt is himself a devout, born-again Christian, belonging to a California fundamentalist group called Church of the Word. His presidency coincided, not by accident, with the presence of hundreds of American missionaries conducting "spiritual work" throughout the countryside. A booklet written by a member of one of these groups declared that, with the coming to power of Ríos Montt, a miracle had occurred. It depicted the general as "the saviour of Guatemala." A strong evangelical bond had thus formed to unite Guatemala and the United States, a bond that had a far greater impact on the lives of ordinary Guatemalans than more formal aspects of U.S. foreign policy.

Another feature of Ríos Montt's presidency was a massive confidence-raising campaign to convince citizens long accustomed to graft and corruption that such things belonged to the past and had no place in a Guatemala governed by him. The government required state employees, from post-office clerks to treasury officials, from high-ranking generals to village policemen, to swear an oath of honesty in which they publicly declared: "I do not steal. I do not lie. I do not abuse my office." Beneath posters announcing that "this government has a commitment to change" (the posters appeared in public agencies throughout Guatemala on January 3, 1983) a legend proclaimed:

For years dishonest authorities, as their own property, have taken money, goods, and resources that do not belong to them.

For years the rule has been that the government and authorities distort the truth, tell lies, and do not fulfil their duties. For years officials have believed that their position gives them rights over the rest of the citizenry and that the law is something they need not abide by. All this constitutes stealing, lying, and abuse of office. It must not continue. Our government has pledged a commitment to change. Respect this commitment yourself. Change!

Another poster forming part of the same campaign depicted a smiling Indian boy with the caption: "For me, you have a commitment to change." Yet another, of a well-groomed brother and sister dressed not in Indian but in Ladino clothes, declared: "For your family and for Guatemala, you have a commitment to change." The change that Ríos Montt championed most, it seems, was a change of heart, which he espoused with unbridled passion during Sunday evening television broadcasts.

Watching and listening to him, I found myself bombarded by questions. Is this man evil? If so, on what grounds? Because he himself directly sanctioned the slaughter of his fellow Guatemalans? How could he? Is he not a Christian? Isn't he a son, a husband, a father who appreciates the value of life? Does he know about the massacres but cannot prevent his troops, for whatever reason, from committing them? Can such awful deeds be done without him, as commander-in-chief of the armed forces, knowing or being told? Has the bloodbath been planned from above, or is it the work of soldiers in the field, gone mindlessly out of control? With whom does responsibility and the burden of truth ultimately rest?

I am still unable to answer these questions. I can, however, volunteer a few points of information about Ríos Montt's presidency with some degree of confidence. By the early part of 1983 violence had decreased, not just in towns and cities but also in the countryside. A drop in the number of killings, however, was interpreted by Washington, far too prematurely, as further evidence that the United States was now dealing with a more responsible government. The Reagan administration went so far as to recommend to Congress that Guatemala be taken off President Carter's human rights "black list," thus enabling military and economic assistance to be resumed.

If, in relative terms, peace prevailed, it was an uneasy, unsettling peace—the peace of the dead. When this peace was shattered it was often difficult to determine the identity and motives of those involved. Rural confrontations were especially murky. Was the cause of an incident the army taking action against an Indian community that would not co-operate and set up civil defence patrols? Could it perhaps be attributed to guerrillas returning to teach a lesson to communities that *had* set up civil defence patrols? Or was the source of conflict one in which old scores were settled—say, over ownership of land, access to a tract of forest, or the right to draw water from a certain stream—under cover of insurgency or the dutiful execution of army orders?

Like all countries in turmoil, Guatemala does not inspire easy answers, except, perhaps, to the chosen likes of Efraín Ríos Montt. In the flux of the moment, however, not even a God-fearing general could have known how long his presidency would last.

# CHAPTER TEN

# Futility at the Polls
## (1984)

M Y TWO WEEKS passed quickly. Visiting Guatemala for such a short time is by no means ideal, but it is better than nothing. Ríos Montt is gone, ousted in August 1983 by a coup that saw General Oscar Mejía Víctores assume the presidency. But the violence continues. To the twenty-seven thousand killings under the Lucas García regime, and an estimated ten thousand under Ríos Montt, must now be added thousands more under Mejía Víctores.

An editorial in the February 23 issue of *El Gráfico* has this to say:

### The Violence Has to End

There is fear among the people over the increase in violence that has been manifest the past several weeks. It is feared that a resurgence of violence may influence the process of democratization, a process that will pass through a crucial stage in the form of an election, called for July 1, to designate members for a National Constituent Assembly. Fear reigns because no one knows what will be the consequences of this new wave of violence, one that has claimed many lives in a short space of time.

Several people have been kidnapped or killed in the last few days alone. The image invoked by General Ríos Montt during his spell in the presidency—"no more bodies on the roadside"— has lost all meaning. Many are the bodies found along highways and thrown down ravines. Many are the Guatemalans—professionals, students, workers, farmers—who are kidnapped in broad daylight in the middle of the street, in full public view of a helpless and terrorized citizenry. Many are the Guatemalans who are abducted from their homes under cover of darkness. Many are the wives, many are the mothers, many are the children who appear in court with the personal effects of their missing relatives, demanding to know their whereabouts. And many also are the people who visit the morgues in an attempt to identify, in the features of the dead, the face of a loved one who has vanished.

This editorial was followed, on March 2, by another equally as frank:

### The Kidnappings Must Cease

Kidnapping as a political weapon or as a means of attaining financial reward is deplorable from any point of view. Many Guatemalans, among them university professors and students, have been kidnapped during the past few weeks in a renewed outbreak of violence that is sweeping the country. The number of these victims has multiplied at an alarming rate. Of the victims, very few have been fortunate enough to show up alive; many have yet to reappear alive or dead. Anguish spreads through the homes of the disappeared, inflicting pain on an impotent citizenry that witnesses the spectacle of violence without being able to do anything about it.

The incidence of these kidnappings, which occur with an elaborate display of force in broad daylight, indicates the degree to which violence has escalated. The citizenry is frightened. It feels insecure and has lost all trust. Guatemala has been afflicted for many years by a lack of security and by a feeling of defencelessness on the part of its population. If these kidnappings and murders persist, peacemaking will be impossible and we will continue to represent, in the eyes of the world, a country where human rights are violated and where the lives of ordinary people are simply not respected.

As well as outspoken editorial opinion, *El Gráfico* ran stories in February and March that highlight the situation. In one episode a group of armed men disguised as doctors abducted the victim of an assassination attempt from a hospital. A single page in the February 23 issue of *El Gráfico* documented the kidnapping of thirty-eight Indians from communities in the highlands, reported the discovery of the beaten and bullet-ridden body of a university professor, and described a shoot-out in downtown Guatemala City. On March 2 *El Gráfico* also reported that the man in charge of overseeing the July 1 elections, Arturo Herbruger Asturias, had received threats against his life for assuming the presidency of the Supreme Electoral Tribunal.

Back in Canada a report prepared by the Inter-Church Committee on Human Rights in Latin America (ICCHRLA) revealed the gravity of the situation. Presented on June 12 to External Affairs Minister Allan MacEachen, the ICCHRLA report states:

> In the case of Guatemala, the internal human rights situation remains the most serious in Central America. Through recent IC-CHRLA visits and through the testimony of refugees, including an escapee from a clandestine prison now resident in Canada, details of torture, kidnappings, detentions, and disappearances in the thousands during the early part of 1984 have been recorded. Continued massacres in the countryside, and of the responsibility of the armed forces themselves for these violations, have been documented by ICCHRLA in conversations with religious personnel working in several areas of Guatemala. The refugee flow and the weight upon Mexico in particular continue to be matters of priority humanitarian concern. The more than seventy documented incursions by Guatemalan military forces into Mexico, including the April 30 attack on a refugee camp several kilometres inside Mexico resulting in grotesque tortures and deaths, should provoke strong international reaction.

Under such circumstances, I ask myself, what difference could an election make? How many people are likely to cast ballots, and who will they be voting for? Is a National Constituent Assembly likely to improve the situation after the election is over?

The July 1 vote turns out to be Guatemala's first major electoral event since the abortive presidential campaign of March 7, 1982. Rampant fraud in the course of that election precipitated a military coup two weeks later, bringing Ríos Montt to power. No elections were held during his fourteen-month presidency. Now some 2.5 million registered voters are being asked to choose among 1,179 candidates representing no fewer than seventeen political parties.

On first inspection, such figures suggest a healthy degree of involvement, but this impression is misleading: no left-of-centre parties are represented. Right-wing groups predominate, among them the Anti-Communist Unification Party and the Authentic Nationalist Party. One contender is General Angel Aníbal Guevara, declared the "winner" of the fraudulent presidential election of 1982. (Although he was president-elect, Guevara never assumed office because of the junior officers' coup of March 23 that same year.) Another contender is General Carlos Manuel Arana, a former president known as the "Butcher of Zacapa" because of his handling of an insurgency threat in eastern Guatemala in the 1960s. An election is irrelevant, for all options represent a continuation of the status quo, not an attempt to change it.

The greatest danger in the July 1 election lies in the possibility of it being perceived as an opportunity for the United States to integrate Guatemala more fully into its plans for Central America as a whole. If the White House greets the election results with approval, if Mejía Víctores then responds to Washington's call for Guatemala to assume a more central regional role in the U.S. isthmian agenda, the only guarantee for the Guatemalan people is even greater repression than they already experience. In this regard, the response of the Reagan Administration is crucial.

As for Canada, Ottawa's position towards Guatemala has been one of increasing detachment and censure, beginning in 1982 with the suspension of bilateral aid. With respect to Central America in general, Canada has moved to distance itself from the ahistorical stance of the United States, even if, in the words of analyst Tim Draimin, Ottawa's policy in the region is "cautious, confused, contradictory, and ineffectual." Canadians concerned about their country's position on Central America can derive some encouragement from a speech delivered in Washington by Maurice Dupras, chairman of the Parliamentary Subcommittee for Canada's Relations with Latin America and the Caribbean.

I testified before the subcommittee in April 1982, and afterwards Dupras solicited my services as a research consultant. I found him to be genuinely affected by the human rights issues that his chairmanship exposed him to, a politician not at all disposed to mince his words. In Washington straight talking was very much in evidence when Dupras told his U.S. audience:

> It hardly needs to be said that it is Washington, not Moscow, that has been for many decades the dominant outside power south of the Río Grande, and nowhere more so than in Central America. Washington's policies in the region closest to it have produced a bloody shambles rather than the intended result of social stability and political acquiescence. There is no area of the world more ripe for revolutionary change. This is the case despite decades during which the United States has not hesitated to employ its immense military, economic, and political influence in the region. Yet, when challenged, President Reagan's stock response is to resort to ideological formulas. History notwithstanding, he reaffirms his simple belief that "the Soviet Union underlies all the unrest that is going on." Progress toward needed reforms will be very difficult without a fundamental change in the attitude of the U.S. government. That means putting faith in the people rather than in military oligarchs with blood on their hands.

In stressing the need for the United States to assist, not subvert, the process of change, Dupras strikes at the heart of the problem. Discontent in Central America springs from generations of poverty and injustice, not a phantom Soviet presence. Nowhere is this more apparent than in Guatemala. Not until the United States understands that what people in Guatemala struggle for is the same cause Americans themselves fought for two centuries ago will peace and stability be possible.

# CHAPTER ELEVEN

# Civilian Rule (1985–86)

I ARRIVED in Guatemala well ahead of the date set for the run-off election, December 8, 1985. Victory at the polls that day belonged to Vinicio Cerezo Arévalo, who won comfortably with 68 per cent of the popular vote. There was a fiesta feel to election day, at least in Antigua. People swarmed the central plaza even more than they do normally. Bands played. Rockets soared. Firecrackers snapped. The returning officers I spoke with were cordial and relaxed, answering questions and even posing for photographs. When it was announced next day that Cerezo had won, people expressed hope that the coming of a new civilian president, not a military one, would signal a new beginning.

I was not so sure. On my flight to Guatemala I had read an interview with Cerezo in *Time* magazine. Cerezo himself appeared to have no illusion about the task at hand. "If I win," he said, "during the first six months I'll have 30 per cent of the power. In the first two years I'll have 50 per cent, and I'll never have more than 70 per cent of the power during my five-year term." How he arrived at these figures was never made clear, but Cerezo's presumably well-informed reckoning was echoed by the Archbishop of Guatemala City, Próspero Penados del Barrio, who remarked: "Whoever becomes president is going to have to move with great caution. You cannot have a dialogue with the armed forces."

The pragmatism of the heads of both church and state is revealing. It is derived, in large part, from their awareness of a structure put in place in Guatemala called the National System of Interinstitutional Co-ordination. Set up by the army as a device by which to monitor political decision-making, this framework ensures continued military involvement in running the country, from mundane local affairs to issues that affect Guatemala on the national and international stage. The hold on political life that the armed forces have exerted for decades will not be relinquished. Instead, certain powers will be entrusted to a civilian administration allowed only to operate within a clearly defined governmental space.

The process of democratization, moreover, is unlikely to unfold in Guatemala in the same way as it has elsewhere in Latin America. Past deeds, from plunder of the national treasury to the wilful practice of terror and intimidation, are unlikely to be held accountable. Unlike, say, General Viela or General Galtieri in Argentina, former presidents Lucas García, Ríos Montt, and Mejía Víctores, all military rulers, will be safe from prosecution as the individuals ultimately responsible for horrific acts of war and gross violation of human rights. One of the last decrees passed by Mejía Víctores before he left office was to grant members of the armed forces immunity from civilian trial for their role in counterinsurgency operations.

Cerezo's star, for the moment, is on the rise. He enjoys immense popularity, ran a well-organized campaign, and won an election that, by Guatemalan standards, was honest and free of fraud. A brave and lucky man who has survived numerous attempts on his life, Cerezo is well aware of the danger of moderate politics in a land where extremes are the norm. He advocates peace talks with the Unidad Revolucionaria Nacional Guatemalteca (URNG), an umbrella organization representing various factions of the insurgent left. During a brief visit to Washington after his election, Cerezo claimed that his government would delay requests from the United States for up to $10 million in military aid already budgeted for Guatemala.

Economic aid is likely to be a different matter. Counterinsurgency war has had a disastrous effect on an economy that, hitherto, was reasonably healthy and well-managed, if massively subsidized by underpaid local labour. Capital flight, an increase in joblessness and underemployment, rising inflation, falling productivity, and decreases in the value of traditional export crops have meant severe economic contraction that only a resumption of full-scale assistance from the United States can alleviate. While a $2.3 billion foreign debt appears minuscule in comparison to what Mexico or Brazil owe to international bankers, unless terms are renegotiated interest payments alone will absorb 40 per cent of Guatemala's annual export earnings.

Repayment of the national debt, however, remains a concept alien to the concerns of most poor Guatemalan families. For Maya Indians in particular, there is primarily the hope that, after years of destruction, life in the highlands may return to its ancient seasonal rhythm.

──────────

It had been years since I had felt it was safe enough to travel in the countryside, but after the election I took advantage of the opportunity to do so, visiting towns and villages I knew and remembered well from the days before repression. I rented a pick-up truck in Guatemala City and headed west and north across the highlands as far as San Mateo Ixtatán. One of my graduate students travelled with me. North of Huehuetenango we were stopped at road blocks and questioned either by civil defence patrols or by the army. None of these checks caused any problems, but they reminded us to be careful. We had to show our passports and prove who we were. We also had to say where we were going and why we wanted to go there.

Along the way I stopped the pick-up once in a while to offer people a ride. Our passengers were predominantly Indians, who climbed in the back with chickens, pigs, an occasional goat, and assorted bundles and baskets. When we dropped them off they were grateful at not having to pay, which allowed us the possibility of conversation. Men did most of the talking; women as a rule were taciturn and wary. The children who accompanied them were invariably silent, save for the odd infant wanting to be fed. Most of the people we spoke with commented repeatedly that, *"primero a Dios,"* thanks be to God, their situation had improved considerably since the early 1980s. They told us they enjoyed freer access to their fields and that both government forces and guerrilla units swept through their communities less and less frequently.

While these people are disposed always to make the best of what life has to offer, around them hang impenetrable memories of suffering and loss. The army bears most responsibility for the slaughter unleashed on them, but guerrilla insurgents are not without blame. Especially in the Sierra de Chuacús and across the northern reaches of the

Sierra de los Cuchumatanes, Indians suffered badly when the Guerrilla Army of the Poor retreated in the face of sustained army offensives, leaving behind unarmed villagers to bear savage reprisal for having provided food, shelter, or moral support for the insurgent cause.

The Saturday before Christmas found us walking around Sacapulas, a town in the Department of El Quiché. We had earlier noticed a huge billboard at the entrance to the department capital, Santa Cruz del Quiché:

WELCOME TO EL QUICHÉ!
LAND OF COURAGEOUS MEN
WHERE THE PEOPLE AND THE ARMY
HAVE SAID "NO!"
TO COMMUNIST SUBVERSION

In Sacapulas the army barracks overlooking the town square caught our attention. The soldiers on guard duty couldn't have been more than sixteen or seventeen years of age. A slogan painted on the side of the watchtower declared:

ONLY THOSE WHO FIGHT
HAVE THE RIGHT TO CONQUER
ONLY THOSE WHO CONQUER
HAVE THE RIGHT TO LIVE

At a time of alleged peace and goodwill—a time when not just Christmas but "democracy," in the form of a civilian president, was supposed to be celebrated—the words on the watchtower invoked quite contrary sentiments.

When I passed through Sacapulas again some months later, the declaration was still prominently displayed, even if the soldiers stationed there looked distinctly off-guard playing basketball with some local school girls. A few weeks earlier, in Verapaz, the land of "true peace," a soldier had opened fire across my path when the car that two friends and I were travelling in attempted to pass his slow-moving jeep.

Like the slogan at Sacapulas, that single shot said it all. The army, not a civilian president, rules Guatemala. The army remains in the driving seat, and its finger is still on the trigger.

CHAPTER TWELVE

# A Militarized Society
# (1987–90)

A NUMBER OF PEOPLE told me they had heard the bombs being dropped. I didn't know whether to believe them or not. "Not *that* close to Antigua," I remember thinking. I remained sceptical until I read about it afterwards, confirmed by official military sources.

On Sunday, February 25, 1990—the day the Sandinistas lost the Nicaraguan election—four fighters belonging to the Quetzal Squadron of the Guatemalan Air Force bombed hilly locations in the Guatemalan township of Magdalena Milpas Altas, where the Organization of People in Arms had earlier engaged an army patrol in combat. The bombing did not take place in some remote, mountain stronghold but in a small community near the old colonial capital, these days a tourist town where Sunday visitors normally fill the central plaza and keep Indian vendors and local merchants busy.

I found Antigua the Sunday following the air raid to be a lot quieter than usual. Visitors stayed away not just because of what had happened in Magdalena Milpas Altas, but because the army and guerrillas had clashed again two days later, in Santa María de Jesús, a township only half-an-hour's bus ride from Antigua and less than fifty kilometres from Guatemala City.

Almost unnoticed by the rest of the world, the war in Guatemala drags dishearteningly on. The army claims that incidents such as those at Magdalena Milpas Altas and Santa María de Jesús (just two of a growing number of confrontations largely unreported outside the country) involve only a small group of "terrorists" left over from the counterinsurgency war of the 1980s. If resistance is so slight, why, one wonders, does the army feel compelled to maintain such a conspicuous presence, not just in and around Antigua but throughout the western highlands? The visibility of the national armed forces, in the countryside most of all, underscores its hold on virtually every aspect of Guatemalan life. The role of the army in civil society, its self-stated vision of what kind of a country Guatemala should be, is worth examining in some detail.

In August 1987, less than a week before the presidents of Central America convened to sign the peace accord known as Esquipulas II, a group known as the Private Enterprise Council of Guatemala organized a "National Forum" that it called "Twenty-Seven Years of Struggle for Liberty." Part of this forum consisted of official presentations by military personnel, with several representatives outlining the army's blueprint for the Guatemala of the future. Counterinsurgency in the 1980s was justified, one official said, "to rescue the nation from subversion and terrorism, a situation that has arisen due to the incompetence of previous governments." The army felt itself, in the words of Colonel Terraza Pinot, "compelled to assume control of the government, so that national dignity could be restored and people's faith in their institutions renewed."

In another speech, General Héctor Gramajo, President Cerezo's Minister of Defence, spelled out how the army views its role as guardian both of democracy and nationhood:

> At this time we consider ourselves to be the institution that gives impetus to democracy. We defend the interests of the nation in its totality, not the interests of a political party, group, or institution. We protect the interests of the nation through political and military action that encompasses all the nation. This action has reciprocal consequences throughout Guatemala.

What General Gramajo means by "reciprocal consequences" is unclear. It may simply be military jargon for fear, harm, and harassment should any priest, lawyer, union representative, or university professor dare to speak out against the army's way of doing things.

One of Gramajo's colleagues, General Manuel Callejas, summed up the army's objectives:

We seek to create a framework of security that permits inte-
grated development in the best of conditions, supporting in all
our greatness the different sectors of the nation, especially the
most needy, focusing the discharge of our duty on achieving
both the supreme national goal and the common good.

The "discharge of duty" Callejas refers to can only be exercised by
commanding not just the apparatus of government but all that makes
the country function, socially and economically as well as politically
and psychologically. The army, "the supreme expression of the state,"
could not forge a "national destiny" without first wielding "national
power."

Brigadier General Juan Bolaños elaborates on the military's concept of power:

Power signifies survival, the ability to impose on others the
methods and procedures of life appropriate for their welfare and
mutual understanding. It is the capacity to enforce the law on
those who lack it, and the ability to extract concessions from the
opponent whom one has defeated.

The "concessions" the brigadier general speaks of have been
extracted at a criminally high price.

What all this rhetoric amounts to, after heartbreak and misery, is
proper recognition that it is the national armed forces, not the Christian Democrat Party of President Cerezo, that are the effective bro-
kers of power in Guatemala. Cerezo has failed his country miserably
by not even attempting to dismantle the national security state devised and maintained by the army. Assuming presidential office in
Guatemala under the circumstances that Cerezo did allowed for little
political manoeuvring, but few Guatemalans could have imagined
when they voted for them that the Christian Democrats would
achieve so pathetically little. Rather than create its own ideas and
pave the way for meaningful social change, Cerezo's government has
absorbed, or has been absorbed by, the military's agenda.

As long ago as the 1970s, the Christian Democrats drew closer to
the military in a move that, the following decade, resulted in the
emergence of a "strategic alliance." Cerezo himself, then the secretary general of the Christian Democracy Party, helped forge this

marriage of convenience, the outcome of which is politics as the continuation of war. In 1975 Cerezo declared:

> Instead of regarding the army as an enemy of the democratic parties, we ought to consider accepting it as an ally of these parties. What I am suggesting is that progressive politicians and military officers have a common responsibility and that both sectors ought to share in the making of national decisions.

Cerezo now speaks of "national reorganization" and the need "to bury the past" in order to attain "national reconciliation." Overall, his tenure as president has been a major disappointment; his last year in office has been one in which human rights violations again made Guatemala an international pariah. How can people "forget the past" when its horrors are part of the present, when the nightmare haunts them still?

Criticism of the Cerezo government's record came in January 1990 from bishops of the Catholic Church when they met in Quezaltenango, Guatemala's second largest city. The bishops published a communiqué that expressed alarm over recent political violence "that has struck at leaders, students, workers, and members of popular organizations." Their statement read: "Human rights, such as the right to dignity and equality, do not exist." They pointed to the injustice inherent in "the traditional structure of a minority that accumulates wealth and privilege while the impoverished majority lacks food, good health, education, and reasonably paid labour."

Episcopal concerns were later reinforced by the United Nations Commission for Human Rights at its 46th session held in Geneva in March 1990. After reviewing the evidence, compiled by both national and international experts, the commission declared itself "profoundly disturbed that the [Guatemalan] government has been unable to control an ongoing climate of violence." It urged Cerezo's government "to initiate or intensify investigations that will allow identification and judicial prosecution of those responsible for acts of torture, disappearances, assassinations, and extra-legal executions." The commission also called for the apprehension of members of acknowledged death squads. It was particularly concerned with what it termed the "grave situation that has affected native peoples from time immemorial." Maya Indians, the commission said, were "the object of discrimination and exploitation, as well as suffering serious violation of their human rights and fundamental liberties."

The disapproval of the Catholic bishops and the United Nations Commission on Human Rights were damning enough, but an even more embarrassing censure came from the U.S. ambassador to Guatemala, Thomas F. Stroock. Addressing the Rotary Club of Guatemala, Ambassador Stroock commented that he found it extraordinary that none of those guilty of kidnapping and killing had yet been brought to justice.

The ambassador's remarks were followed by the release of a hard-hitting report compiled not by Amnesty International or Americas Watch but by the U.S. Department of State. In it the United States (which has furnished Cerezo's government with $800 million in aid) observed that a deteriorating human rights situation in 1989 had taken the lives of over two thousand Guatemalans. Their deaths were attributed, among other causes, to the activities of "ultra-right groups" and "military personnel" involved in "extrajudicial killing." President Cerezo dismissed the report, which considers Guatemala to be among a handful of countries across the world "plagued by insurgency, civil unrest, and terrorism," as "false press information." Cerezo's comment, in turn, prompted the release of another State Department bulletin, which noted "the disturbing increase in what appears to be politically related violence."

There is no small, tragic irony in this exchange of words, for the architects of U.S. foreign policy in the 1990s only have their colleagues of forty years ago to thank for cultivating a military caste that has brought so much grief to the people of Guatemala.

# CHAPTER THIRTEEN

# The Daily News
# (1990)

I MAKE MY WAY to my favourite table, in the corner of the patio where the light is good, and start to read. The waitress brings me coffee and smiles. She hovers, nods at the papers, and asks, "Don't you ever get tired of all that news?"

It is the summer of 1990, the time of year they call winter in Guatemala on account of the rains. I am here for several months, working with a translator on turning the English text of a book of mine into a Spanish-language edition. It is a slow, tedious process; sometimes progress is made not even sentence by sentence, but word by word. Reading the newspapers, by comparison, constitutes something of a break.

"Not really," I reply. "I like to know what's going on."

"Nobody I know reads the newspapers as much as you do," she says. "They find them too upsetting. Besides, they don't have the time."

She leaves me to ponder our exchange. For better or worse, I *do* have the time. By summer's end I have accumulated a larger pile of newspaper clippings than usual.

---

Two items from *El Gráfico* of June 11 help put the country in social, economic, and political context. The first, with the headline "Guatemala: 6.4 Million Impoverished People," says:

With nine million inhabitants, Guatemala reflects a state of poverty that embraces 71 per cent of its population, a statistic that classifies the country as the worst-off in this regard in all of Central America, according to a report released by the Instituto de Nutrición de Centroamérica y Panamá (INCAP). Data from INCAP reveals that poverty most seriously afflicts people living in rural areas, where the index pertains to 83.7 per cent of residents, the index for urban areas being 47 per cent. INCAP's figures lend support to the findings of the latest national survey of socio-demographic conditions, in which it was found that 83 per cent of Guatemalan families live in poverty.

Further analysis, specifically of families considered in dire need, shows that 64 per cent of them earn 251 *quetzales* ($59 U.S.) or less each year. Poverty is most chronic, according to the national survey, in the northwestern departments of Huehuetenango and El Quiché, where 91.5 per cent of families are affected.

The second item, under the headline "Guatemala: 40,000 disappeared," summarizes the proceedings of the "First National Seminar on the Effectiveness of Habeas Corpus." Held in the civilized ambience of the Sheraton Conquistador Hotel, the seminar was reported by *El Gráfico* as revealing that "more than half of the 90,000 political disappearances that have occurred in Latin America in recent years relate to Central America." The reporter covering the seminar further notes that most of the Central American cases involve Guatemala, "where more than 40,000 disappearances have been recorded and where no explanation has been given to the thousands of families who suffer on account of this phenomenon." What the reporter failed to note is that no member of the government who had earlier promised to attend the seminar (representatives of the Supreme Court, the Ministry of Justice, and the Human Rights Office) actually showed up to discuss matters with members of non-governmental and international agencies who did.

A couple of weeks later, on June 27, a story on the human rights situation appeared in the *Prensa Libre*, a Guatemalan newspaper whose official motto advocates journalism that is "independent, honourable, and dignified." Careful to attribute what it states to the wire services of the Mexican daily *El Excelsior*, the story in the *Prensa Libre* runs:

According to the [UN] Commissioner for Human Rights in Central America, Guatemala heads the list of countries in that region in violation of human rights. With the coming to power of President [Vinicio] Cerezo, great expectations were raised that an end would be put to the wave of terrorism unleashed by the military and death squads. But the [Cerezo] regime has been unable to distinguish itself in any way, or to leave behind a human rights record different from that of [military] dictatorships.

*Prensa Libre* continues:

According to statistics provided by the Guatemalan Human Rights Commission, during the time that President Cerezo has held office extralegal executions have taken the lives of two thousand people, while another two thousand have disappeared. Death squads, human rights groups allege, are once again in action, investigating and informing on people, killing them or carrying them off to clandestine prisons where they are subjected to physical and psychological torture. Guatemala is considered the worst violator of human rights in Latin America, for in this country between 1966 and 1990 more than 40,000 people have disappeared, 100,000 have been killed, 75,000 have been widowed, 125,000 have been orphaned, 150,000 have been displaced outside the country, and over one million displaced internally.

----

A good way of gaining perspective on any situation is to compare the present with the past or to contrast what is going on somewhere today with what currently prevails elsewhere. This is the strategy adopted by Carlos Rafael Soto in a biting op-ed piece published by *Siglo Veintiuno* on June 22. Soto takes as his point of departure the spirited performance in the World Cup of one of Guatemala's neighbours, Costa Rica, whose non-professional soccer players disposed of both Scotland and Sweden en route not only to the second round of *mundial* competition but to a hallowed place in Central American memory. Costa Rica's success, in other endeavours as well as at soccer, move Soto to the following reflections:

The victories of Costa Rica in World Cup action make all of us, as Central Americans, feel proud. At the same time, however, they cause to stir within us feelings of jealousy and sadness, not just because of a fine sporting performance but because that fine sporting performance reflects Costa Rican reality, in contrast to the reality in which Guatemalans find themselves.

Back in the 1950s, Guatemala reigned supreme in Central America. In the soccer match that inaugurated Mateo Flores stadium, Guatemala played Colombia as part of the Central American and Caribbean Games. Guatemala won 1-0, thanks to a wonderful goal by Pepino Toledo and some spectacular attacking play by Gabriel Urriola. Students would come from all over Central America to our university. We were still then the undisputed leader of the region, a country where President Arbenz had begun to enact policies which—even his closest rivals would today concede—sought to promote capitalist development, dismantling U.S. monopolies and taking control for ourselves of means of transportation by land and by sea. But that happened forty years ago. Since then all we have to show is four decades of blood-letting, kidnapping, corruption, greed, foreign domination, and a shameful quality of life, which relegate us to a position among the poorest, most backward nations on earth.

Soto goes on to list an array of statistics that show how much better off Costa Ricans are than Guatemalans, whether the difference is measured in terms of food consumption, rates of infant mortality, or access to education. He attributes Costa Rica's advances in social welfare, as well as its ability to play soccer in Italy with the best of the world, to imaginative and responsible leadership. Soto elaborates:

A case in point is the peace process in Central America. The original idea was Vinicio Cerezo's, but the Nobel Peace Prize went to [Oscar] Arias. Why? Because Arias understood better his role as political and moral leader of his country, because Arias was sufficiently patriotic to resist the temptation to fill his government with personal friends, because Arias knew how to construct a respectable image. In Guatemala the opposite occurred. What happened to Costa Rica during the World Cup in Italy, therefore, is not an isolated incident. It is the natural outcome of a people who live in relative tranquillity, who know their institutions are functioning more or less adequately, who have confidence that their social services as well as their health and education facilities are properly run. These people know that when they are born an opportunity awaits them, that it will be possible for them to go to school, that it will be possible for them to eat well enough so as not to fall victim to the malnutrition that plagues Guatemalan school children in second and third grade. These people know, furthermore, that the rules of politics have been established and respected for some time, that they need not live in fear of a fraudulent election, a military coup, or crippling pillage of public funds.

Soto's disgust at the corrupt, self-serving ways of Guatemalan politics, and his disappointment that civilian president Vinicio Cerezo has done no better in this regard than the colonels and generals who preceded him, are sentiments commonly shared and expressed. Cerezo's presidency is destined to be remembered as one of opportunity lost. To be sure, his options were limited from the start. If, as most observers acknowledge, radical change was not part of the Christian Democrat agenda, the opportunity at least existed for the president to set a respectful example. This might have been achieved by exercising what Soto identifies as "moral" leadership, making sound decisions not only in public but in private life as well, decisions that would perhaps restore some faith to Guatemalans long accustomed to broken promises that civilian presidents conduct themselves differently than military ones.

Cerezo's reputation has suffered badly as a result of several tactless actions, including the purchase of a private Mediterranean island also sought by singer Julio Iglesias. It was the singer's disenchantment at the sale not going his way that moved him to investigate and disclose the name of his competitor.

Whether or not Cerezo will retire to his private island after serving out his term, he will be able to set sail for the Mediterranean in his private yacht, as he did in July, following his return from meetings in Mexico with President Carlos Salinas de Gortari. *Siglo Veintiuno* notes on July 21 that Cerezo, rather than returning and facing any number of domestic crises, "went down to the Pacific to embark on a pleasure trip aboard his yacht Odyssey, with the likeli-hood of sailing beyond Central American territory." In a thinly veiled reference to the president's notorious womanizing, *Siglo Veintiuno* also notes, "It is not known who is accompanying him." His wife, apparently, was not aboard.

―――――――――――

Cerezo's purpose in going to Mexico was to discuss with President Salinas the fate of thousands of Guatemalans, most of them Maya Indians, who fled to Mexico in the early 1980s to escape political violence in their homeland. Living in Mexico for up to ten years, these families have built homes, seen children born, and forged new ties. They have refused government offers of repatriation and reset-tlement, maintaining that those who return to Guatemala live there in fear of persecution. The "solution" to the "problem" now being proposed is to grant refugees and their offspring status as Mexican residents or citizens.

An editorial in *La Hora* of July 18 addresses the plight of the refugees:

> One has to understand that the trauma caused by violence to these thousands of Guatemalans will not disappear overnight but will, in many cases, leave scars that can never heal. We must remember that Guatemalan Indians found themselves, literally, in the crossfire between the guerrillas and the army, caught in a national conflict in which the innocent and the anonymous were the principal victims. The most extreme action to which these people sought recourse was in the long march overland to Mexico, where they settled in search of peace and security. The existence of these refugees serves as a permanent reminder to our national conscience, telling us that we must never again allow events to happen that cause people to abandon the land of their ancestors.
>
> We must comprehend, furthermore, that Indian customs and traditions are rooted in the land of their forefathers. That the pressures to leave were so great that they swept aside such attachments and values is made only more extreme by the fact that most of those who left have no desire to return, doubtless

fearful that if they did come back they might relive the nightmare they have already experienced.

––––––––––––

Any refugee who fled Guatemala in the early 1980s and is pondering
government appeals to return and resume normal life will find in the
body counts reported daily good reason to stay away. It is simply not
possible to document all incidents of assassination or disappearance.
It is equally impossible to ascribe plausible motives to many of the
atrocities brought to public notice by the press. If details concerning
the reasons behind acts of violence are absent or vague, not so are
some of the circumstances that reporters encounter when they are
sent to investigate wrongdoing. What they discover or are told is
often written up in cold, alienated prose, as if the victim's sole purpose in life was to be, in death, so casually and unsympathetically
described.

The gory weekly *Extra* specializes in this sort of horror, but the
mainstream dailies are not above depicting a violent end to human
life in language devoid of all semblance of emotion. The glib
detachment of the following items, from *El Gráfico* of June 28, is not
easy to render, but translated from icy, eviscerated Spanish (the
headings are as they appear in the original), the notices run something like this:

### A Crime in Atitlán

Violence in Santiago Atitlán has intensified of late. Now it is
reported that a crime has been perpetrated against Sebastián Bal-
tasar Vásquez, eighteen years of age. He was cut down by delin-
quents who opened fire on him with automatic weapons. His
body was taken to the morgue at the national hospital in Sololá.

### This Time in Zone Two

An unknown man was killed by five gunshots when he was
walking down Second Street in Zone Two, so it was revealed
when law officers arrived at the scene of the crime. The victim
carried no identification but it was explained that the five gunshots his body received were of varying calibres, indicating that
he was attacked by more than one person.

### One More in El Campanero

A man yet to be identified was shot to death by the occupants of three vehicles, who dumped his body in the district of Guatemala City known as El Campanero. Someone who observed the killing disclosed to the authorities that the assassins numbered at least eight and that they arrived and left in three different vehicles.

### A Woman

A change of gender, but the act is the same. A woman was strangled to death at the corner of Twenty-Second Avenue and Twenty-Seventh Street in Zone Five, after she was assaulted by a gang of thugs. As of yesterday she had not been identified. Her body may be found in the Autopsy Hall in Zone Three.

---

Guatemala's land is rich and fertile, yet its people are hungry and poor. The country whose first agriculturalists domesticated and harvested corn now has to import it from the United States. The paradox is disconcerting.

Perhaps the greatest irony of all is that in Guatemala a group of scientists laid claim to medical history with their successful experiments in finding a substitute for human blood, one that apparently can be used in any transfusion without the complications created by the age of AIDS. A country where blood is routinely spilled hopes to become known as a country where life can be saved, not brutally taken. A feature from *Siglo Veintiuno* on June 8 reports:

> Guatemalan researchers have made a major breakthrough that will allow transfusions of animal blood to be used to save human lives. Doctors from our country will soon become famous for their sensational discovery of a substitute for human blood, a compound consisting of blood extracted from calves mixed with other clinical ingredients. Known as *Hemopure*, the compound can be used on human beings. Its discovery marks an important step in the history of medicine, one of benefit to all humankind.
>
> Guatemalan scientists Rodolfo Herrera Llerandi, Rodolfo García-Gallont, Erika von der Goltz, Ruediger von der Goltz,

Edgar López, and the American doctor William Trainor carried out a series of tests in laboratories at the Herrera Llerandi private hospital to determine the precise extent to which the special compound works on human patients. The most essential feature of the discovery is that animal blood taken from calves contains no RH elements and is not group specific, meaning that it is a common blood, one that can be put into any living person, no matter what that person's blood type happens to be.

A hospital spokesman, Dr. Dagoberto Sosa Montalvo, expressed his enthusiasm at the discovery, pointing out that transfusions henceforth could be done without exposing patients to hepatitis or AIDS. The first person to receive the calf-blood compound was in fact Dr. Rodolfo García-Gallont, who was subjected to intensive scrutiny for twenty-four hours after the transfusion was undertaken. During observation his organism showed no sign of complications. Laboratory tests also proved positive and normal. Nine other volunteer doctors were similarly treated and tested.

As well as being suitable for all blood groups, the substitute is easily manufactured and can be kept in refrigeration until needed. In future it will be possible to carry out transfusions without beforehand testing for blood type, thus saving valuable time during an emergency.

*Hemopure*, the substitute for human blood, is the outcome of co-operation between Guatemalan doctors supported by the Biopure Corporation of Boston, Massachusetts, the Guatemalan company Laboratorios Biopur, and its parent company Hemo-Innovations. This historic landmark in the annals of Guatemalan and world medicine will be made public in a special ceremony at the United Nations.

––––––––––

June 30 is Army Day in Guatemala, complete with a parade passing through the downtown streets of the capital. The armed forces consider themselves the guardians of the nation, the only institution that can be relied upon to keep at bay the virulent cancer of communism. No better spectacle exists to showcase just how militarized Guatemalan society has become than the Army Day parade. If a trip

to Ixil country and a tour of "model villages" there fail to convince
the foreign visitor of the army's pervasive authority, then observing
the extent to which civil defence patrols figured in the 1990 com-
memoration certainly would have. Watching seasoned counterinsurgency units march past in full combat regalia or contemplating
the manipulation involved in getting Maya recruits to turn out in
traditional community attire also imparts a sense of the mountain
that guerrilla forces fight in vain to move. *El Gráfico* of July 1 cap-
tures the scene:

> With the presence of historic battalions and a dense column of
> civil defence members, the parade commemorating Army Day
> filed past the army high command and its chief officer, President
> Cerezo. From the executive balcony of the national palace, pro-
> tected by three darkened screens of bullet-proof glass, President
> Cerezo watched in the company of Juan Leonel Bolaños, Minis-
> ter of Defence and Head of Division, and generals Juan José
> Marroquín Silezár, Roberto Mata Gálvez, and Raúl Molina
> Bedoya. The army chose yesterday only to put on display small
> components of its manpower and weaponry, giving greater
> emphasis to the participation of reserves and civil defence
> patrols. The loudest cheers were for the Army Corps of Engi-
> neers, in recognition of its work in rural areas of the country.
> Also applauded were the *kaibiles* [counterinsurgency veterans]
> and the parachute brigade. The Guard of Honour had in its
> ranks two children, a boy and a girl, both dressed in army
> fatigues and marching behind flag-carrying escorts. The children
> attracted a lot of attention.

———————

One general not watching the parade from the "executive balcony"
was ex-president Efraín Ríos Montt. Driven from the political lime-
light by a rival faction during the military coup of August 1983, Ríos
Montt is once again in the news. His intention is to run for the presidency in the November elections, even though clause 186(a) of the
Guatemalan constitution prohibits anyone involved in a military
coup, as Ríos Montt was in March 1982, from campaigning for
office. He claims that this clause became law after 1982 and there-

fore does not apply to his case. The Supreme Electoral Tribunal disagrees and has declared Ríos Montt ineligible. It has also responded negatively to an appeal that its decision be reversed. None of this has deterred the general, whose counterinsurgency operations during his fourteen months as president have led human rights activists to suggest that it would be more appropriate for Ríos Montt to be put on trial for crimes against humanity than be considered a candidate for the presidency.

Ríos Montt's high profile has also drawn concern from Archbishop Penados del Barrio, who fears a serious confrontation over religious matters if the general participates in the election, for his evangelical ways (and those of his fanatical hangers-on) undermine popular support for the Catholic Church. When, on the evening of July 12, Congress began to debate Ríos Montt's case, the session had to be suspended after repeated interruptions from the public in attendance. Most civilians present backed Ríos Montt's candidacy and heckled constantly during the proceedings, which were chaired by Guatemalan vice-president Roberto Carpio Nicolle. At one point two congressmen, Oliverio García Rodas and Victor Hugo Godoy, beseeched the crowd for order, only to have hot chile peppers thrown in their eyes. Godoy also had his spectacles seized and trampled on.

According to *Siglo Veintiuno*, when Ríos Montt was asked to comment on the disturbances, he denounced the congressional forum as a charade organized by "sick, mistaken, dirty old fools of men who rape their own daughters." He also warned congressmen, "They can be sure that when I win the elections I will judge them one by one, and will order meticulous investigations to be made into how they managed to spend so much money so quickly." When he was asked "What else would you do if elected?" Ríos Montt replied: "Perhaps I would talk less and do more. I cannot be bought. I am a soldier. I have always been faithful. I have always been honest."

————————

One morning a heavy, persistent rain catches me without an umbrella and keeps me away from the chores of translation longer than I had anticipated. At the café I have long since finished my second cup of coffee—and reading the newspapers. I listen to the downpour and watch it transform the street outside into a flashflood aqueduct. As I wait for the rain to end I notice the waitress concentrating on an issue of *Prensa Libre*.

"Well," I say. "You've found time after all to catch up on the news."

"No," she answers. "I'm just checking the lottery numbers."

# CHAPTER FOURTEEN

# The Fiction of Democracy
## (1991)

A T CHIMALTENANGO, fifty-five kilometres west of Guate-mala City, the Pan American Highway becomes a desolate strip of bars, night clubs, gambling joints, and brothels. Branching off the highway, the road to Antigua is lined on both sides by towering stands of eucalyptus. Night is falling as we approach the army base on the outskirts of town. The speed bumps in front of it slow us down to a crawl. A soldier stares at the pick-up as it passes the garrison entrance. I glance behind where he stands to the wall of a building beside the parade ground. Although the light is dim I can still read the words emblazoned on it:

> SOME PEOPLE THINK ABOUT PEACE:
> OUR JOB IS TO WORK FOR IT.

The notion of an army that most observers consider a perpetual vio-lator of human rights billing itself as an agent of peace may seem absurd, but Guatemala abounds in such manipulation. Jorge Serrano Elías, who won the presidential election of January 6, 1991, shows himself no more capable of controlling the national armed forces than his predecessor Vinicio Cerezo. Political killings and intimida-tions continue at an alarming rate, reflecting the civilian govern-ment's inability or fear to investigate, especially if the army is implicated. Failure to investigate crimes and lay charges in a court of law is the norm.

Cerezo's last year in office saw human rights violations in Guatemala continue to be monitored by the U.S. State Department, a source even the most hard-line of generals could hardly link to "communist subversion." The State Department issued a report on July 28, 1991, indicating that, in 1990, six thousand people were assassinated in Guatemala: five hundred a month, fifteen persons a day. Most controversial was the report's willingness to categorize 304 killings as political assassinations. The report attributed blame for these killings directly to the national armed forces or to individuals associated with the national armed forces and therefore protected by them. The report emphasized that the army and also the police are exempt from prosecution in cases of human rights violations, which effectively means that the rule of law operates with serious restriction.

A week before the distribution of the U.S. State Department report, Guatemala's own human rights ombudsman, Ramiro de León Carpio, drew public attention to more than three hundred "extrajudicial killings" between January 1 and June 30, 1991, the first six months of Serrano's presidency. De León Carpio also pointed out that two of every three depositions brought to his attention fell beyond his terms of reference. This made him unwilling to designate Serrano's presidency as one in which, thus far, an improvement could be observed in human rights. Hundreds of killings reported by the local press went without any kind of official inquiry.

De León Carpio's statement did not please members of Serrano's administration. Nor did remarks he made about "unconstitutional" recruitment go over well with the army high command, many of whose rank and file are abducted into service. The outspokenness of someone in De León's position is rare, for far more than most state bureaucrats, he knows the price paid by Guatemalans who dare to challenge the system.

One particularly repugnant assassination was that of agronomist Julio Quevedo Quezada, murdered in front of his wife and children by two gunmen while on his way to visit his parents in Santa Cruz del Quiché. Quevedo was a prominent member of the Catholic relief agency CARITAS. His shooting provoked strong condemnation from both Bishop Julio Cabrera of El Quiché and Monseñor Próspero Penados del Barrio, Archbishop of Guatemala City. Penados lashed out at the impunity that the culprits of the deed would enjoy. "Crimes such as this are never resolved," he said, "for the authorities always tell us they will investigate and everything ends right there, which means the identity of the killers is never determined nor is anyone apprehended."

Having the will to prosecute means taking enormous risks, as lawyer Roberto Arturo Lemus can attest. He, like Quevedo, also worked in El Quiché, where he represented Maya Indians who wished to bring to trial members of a civil defence patrol accused of the murder and harassment of fellow community residents. Shortly after overseeing the necessary legal proceedings, Lemus and his family received multiple death threats. On July 15, 1991, Lemus left Guatemala for exile in Canada.

Human rights violations have become so serious that the United States has once again decided to suspend all military aid and to impose conditions on programs of economic assistance. These actions were taken after Serrano refused to have disbursements of military aid tied to improvements in human rights. Thus a non-military package amounting to $56.5 million in 1990 was cut to $30 million for 1991. This reduction has served to cool relations between the two countries considerably and has worsened the already dismal plight of the Guatemalan economy. Surveys of working conditions by local and international agencies reckon that 65 per cent of the economically active population is underemployed, that three out of every four workers earn wages of only $2.50 (Canadian) daily. These starvation incomes mean mass poverty.

Mass poverty assumes the spectre of a medical nightmare with the arrival in Guatemala of cholera. In an odd geographical diffusion, the disease entered Guatemala not (as expected) from the south but from the north, moving "down" from Mexico as opposed to "up" through Central America from Peru (the country of origin), Ecuador, and Colombia. The first confirmed case was that of Gabriel Zacarias Méndez, a resident of San Marcos who had returned to Guatemala after a period of work on a farm in the Mexican state of Chiapas.

Zacarias was admitted to hospital in Guatemala City on July 21, 1991, and was taken off the critical list four days later following an intensive course of treatment that turned the migrant worker into a temporary celebrity. His expensive, high-tech recovery will not be a fate shared by other Guatemalans. By August 4, sixteen more cases had been confirmed and were being attended to in Coatepeque. A medical alert has been raised, not just in Guatemala but throughout Central America, where doctors estimate six hundred thousand people may eventually be infected, about four thousand of them fatally. The Suchiate River, which forms part of Guatemala's western border with Mexico, has been found to be contaminated, and health officials are clamping down on public eating facilities following a survey reporting that nine of every ten plates of food sold by street vendors contain fecal matter—and there are thirteen thousand street vendors alone in and around Guatemala City. Cholera thrives under such conditions and could become endemic in Guatemala for the remainder of the century.

Serrano, then, presides over Guatemala during a time of ongoing crisis. He deserves some recognition for promoting face-to-face discussions in Mexico with representatives of the guerrilla insurgency, whose combatants have now been waging war against the army for over thirty years. An agreement signed in Querétaro on July 25, 1991, under the auspices of the United Nations, spelled out a common platform relating to issues of "democratization" that many onlookers hope is a prelude to peace talks and a negotiated settlement. Significantly, four signatories for the Guatemalan government were members of the national armed forces. Only if their institution truly decides to work for peace will any prospect of it be possible.

# CHAPTER FIFTEEN

# *Searching for Peace (1993–94)*

HE TENSE DAYS between May 25 and June 5, 1993 saw Ramiro de León Carpio, the country's Human Rights Ombudsman, replace Jorge Serrano Elías as the president of Guatemala. I was working in Spain at the time, but I managed to follow events hour by hour by tuning in to that most dedicated of correspondents, the BBC World Service. The Spanish dailies *El País* and *Diario 16* also kept me informed. An attempt on Serrano's part to seize dictatorial powers appeared at first to have military approval, but senior members of the armed forces distanced themselves from Serrano's manoeuvres and his "constitutional coup" soon aborted. Like Vinicio Cerezo in 1986, De León Carpio enjoyed widespread public support when he assumed the presidency, for as human rights ombudsman he was sharply critical of both the government and the army. As president De León Carpio has seen his popularity drop considerably, and so far his policies have had mixed results.

The most impressive achievement of De León Carpio's first year in office was the signing of a Comprehensive Human Rights Accord on March 29, 1994, during peace negotiations in Mexico City with rebel insurgents of the Unidad Revolucionaria Nacional Guatemalteca (URNG). The discussions had begun with some promise under Serrano in April 1991, but they had turned sour and acrimonious by March 1993, with the government claiming positive outcomes that neither the URNG nor Monseñor Rodolfo Quezada Toruño, President of the Committee for National Reconciliation, could confirm. The URNG was especially troubled by the attitude of Serrano's defence minister, General José Domingo García Samayoa. It accused García Samayoa of making statements that "put in serious risk the continuation of further dialogue." De León Carpio managed to restore faith in the stalled peace talks, culminating in the Human Rights Accord, which in principle represents a major breakthrough.

Several clauses of the accord are noteworthy. Both the government and the URNG acknowledge that "all agreements must be accompanied by appropriate national and international verification." This means, among other things, that the United Nations will be invited "to establish itself and to move freely" throughout Guatemala. A UN delegation led by Leonardo Franco arrived in Guatemala on April 25, 1994, to lay the groundwork for the verification process.

The presence of the United Nations is crucial not only to the implementation of the accord but also as a potential deterrent to Guatemala's heavy-handed security forces, which for years have operated with impunity. The accord explicitly recognizes "the need for firm action against impunity," with the government agreeing not to permit "the adoption of legislative or other kinds of measures designed to prevent the prosecution and punishment of persons responsible for human rights violations." This clause suggests that amnesty legislation favoured by the Guatemalan military will not be pursued. Holding the national armed forces accountable for past actions—they, not the URNG, have committed the worst of atrocities—will be a decisive test of De León Carpio's credibility.

The president himself is in favour of establishing a Truth Commission as a necessary step in forging national reconciliation. The URNG supports him in this view, and both parties are mindful that such investigations helped heal the wounds of war in El Salvador, Chile, and Argentina. The national armed forces are less enthusiastic. De León Carpio's minister of defence, General Mario René Enríquez Morales, has made it clear that the Guatemalan military would only tolerate a Truth Commission that did not identify human rights abusers by name.

In addition to the Human Rights Accord, the government and the URNG signed an agreement outlining a timetable for subsequent negotiations. Its goals are worthy but formidable. Each month between May and November 1994 talks are to address such key issues as the repatriation and resettlement of displaced families, native rights, social and economic improvement, the role of the army in civil society, the transformation of the URNG from a fighting force to a political party, and constitutional and electoral reform. Successful negotiation of these issues commits both parties to signing "a firm and lasting peace agreement."

But even if consensus can be struck, the issues themselves will continue to be thorny. The high-profile return of about 2,500 refugees from Mexico in January 1993 was to have been followed, between May and August that same year, by another 1,600 families, some 8,000 people. Official statistics indicate that by January 1994 less than half that number had moved back to Guatemala from camps in the Mexican states of Chiapas, Campeche, and Quintana Roo. Those who were repatriated often found themselves in a difficult situation, stigmatized by the army and even government officials as guerrilla sympathizers and consequently treated with suspicion or outright hostility by residents of the communities to which they returned or in which they were resettled. Statements by De León Carpio himself linked refugee families to the URNG, an unwarranted association that only serves to perpetuate fear, distrust, and uncertainty.

Native rights are similarly intractable. Any number of social indicators puts Guatemala's six million Maya Indians among the most disadvantaged of its citizens. Statistics concerning access to education are particularly acute. Only one in four primary school students is Maya, with the ratio for secondary participation dropping to one in ten. University-level attendance is even lower: one in twenty. Six of every ten women in Guatemala cannot read or write. Some three-quarters of non-literate women are Maya, whose schooling in rural areas is often basic or non-existent, with only one girl in eight advancing beyond sixth grade. To his credit, De León Carpio named a Maya Indian, Celestino Tay Coyoy, as education minister, but the resources he has to work with are limited and the prejudices of the system he heads entrenched.

Equally entrenched are elite positions with respect to land and landholding. Skewed patterns of land distribution lie at the heart of Guatemala's woes. The country is strikingly agrarian, with the lives of thousands of peasant families and the existence of a privileged elite connected by the politics of land ownership. In Guatemala, 90 per cent of the total number of farms account for 16 per cent of total farm area, while 2 per cent of the total number of farms occupy 65 per cent of total farm area. The best land is used to grow coffee, cotton, bananas, and sugar cane for export, not to feed malnourished local populations. Recent UN statistics indicate that 85 per cent of Guatemalans live in poverty, 70 per cent of them in a state of deprivation described as extreme. Only 15 per cent are considered to live well. They live well not only because they enjoy the fruits of the land but also because lenient taxation laws mean that their contribution to state revenues, in percentage terms, is among the lowest in Latin America. Elite benefits would be enhanced if the government assumes private sector debts, a move that the president of Congress, Vinicio Villar, defended against public outcry.

One of President De León Carpio's most contradictory stands involves the continued existence of civil defence patrols, which exemplify the extent to which Guatemala has become, and remains, a militarized society. Some five hundred thousand men currently perform civil defence duty, a number that the army says it can raise to nine hundred thousand should the need arise. As human rights ombudsman, De León Carpio was a fierce critic of civil defence patrols and advocated that they be dismantled. As president he asserts the need for them to be retained, despite evidence that links the patrols directly with assaults, intimidation, illegal detentions, and assassination, especially in the countryside. Positive steps that saw military personnel purged from the ranks of the police force are therefore offset by the president's reversal on the issue of civil defence patrols. His reversal, not surprisingly, has drawn him closer in allegiance to the army high command that he once spoke out against. The army continues to be the most powerful and best organized institution in Guatemala. Its control of civil defence patrols allows it to exert its influence at the local level in towns and villages throughout the country.

Major obstacles surround the dissolution of the URNG as an armed force and seem certain to retard its emergence as a viable political player on the national scene. Understandably, the URNG is reluctant to demobilize its ranks until all aspects of the Human Rights Accord are operative and guarantees for personal safety are in place. Then begins the delicate business of turning clandestine backing into open support, followed by the mammoth task of convincing voters in a future election to cast their ballots for whatever party the URNG evolves into. If neighbouring El Salvador offers any basis for comparison, the URNG faces an uphill struggle. In El Salvador, the insurgent groups making up the Farabundo Martí National Liberation Front (FMLN) waged a war that ended in stalemate, not in defeat. There, on election day, the FMLN could count on greater public sympathy than the URNG enjoys in Guatemala. If electoral defeat, followed by bitter internal feuding, was the fate of the FMLN, it is difficult to imagine a more encouraging outcome for the URNG.

Also difficult to imagine is politics in Guatemala without some kind of military involvement. The national armed forces, at forty-seven thousand men the largest and most professional military force in Central America, are headed by a corps of officers whose training cultivates politics as a legitimate military preoccupation. For any president of Guatemala, the greatest challenge is to convince the army that civil society, as in the case of Costa Rica, can function reasonably well without the involvement of the military. Peace in Guatemala hinges on defining a very different role for the national armed forces than they have assumed and enacted up to now.

CHAPTER SIXTEEN

---

# How Was Guatemala?

I miss my morning chats with Joselino very much. Even on days when the news he delivers is particularly bad, he has something to say about soccer, the rains, his girlfriends, Antigua gossip, or world affairs that cheers me up. I miss his quirky human touch. The anonymous manner by which *The Globe and Mail* arrives on my front porch does not compare. When I make my way through its pages the trace of Guatemala is as faint as the trace of Canada is there.

Guatemala, I have learned to accept, unfolds in a trajectory of its own elaboration. It has become, for me, a peculiar habit of mind, a metaphor of life and death. The only thing I'm sure of is that its people deserve better than they get. I think of Don Andrés, a retired caretaker, and wonder if the pension the government promised him has in fact come through. I think of José, who shines shoes for a living, and wonder if the money I left with him secured him a place to live. I think of Beto, a tramp who sits outside the Hotel Aurora acknowledging alms with the smile of an angel. I think of the woman in the park who sells *arroz*, a delicious hot drink made of rice, milk, and cinnamon, and wonder if inflation will cause her to raise the price of a glass another five or ten *centavos*. I think of the nuns at San Cristóbal Totonicapán, and wonder how the medicine they distribute is holding up.

How was Guatemala? I'll know better next time I visit.

# PART THREE

# Spaniards, Ladinos, and Maya Resistance

# CHAPTER SEVENTEEN

# The Colonial Experience

UNLIKE native peoples elsewhere in the Americas, whose memory belongs to history, whose trace on the earth is faint, the Maya of Guatemala are very much a living culture. They sustain a presence no visitor to the country can fail to notice, can avoid being struck by. I recall how unusual I felt the first time I realized that I was the odd one out, travelling alone in a busload of Indians north of Huehuetenango.

Even modern government censuses, which enumerate fewer Mayas than there actually are, record sizeable native populations: 1 million in 1893, 1.6 million in 1950, and 3 million in 1973. Today, six million strong, Mayas are challenging the Guatemalan state as never before, pressing for community autonomy, lobbying for land and language rights, and articulating the cause of self-determination with canny, characteristic persistence. Anthropologists now speak of a Maya nationalist movement emerging in Guatemala, a development that has given a decidedly cultural dimension to political struggle.

Who are these peoples? How, through the centuries, have they managed to survive? What sorts of lives have they lived? Why should their lot concern us? These questions have charged my research interests for some time: I am inspired by the stand made by Spaniards like Bartolomé de las Casas, a Dominican friar who championed native rights in the sixteenth century; I am moved by the courage of Rigoberta Menchú, the Maya woman whose award of the Nobel Peace Prize in 1992 focused international attention on more recent burdens, more recent iniquities, more recent threats to survival.

Survival itself is the fundamental issue, but one we must tackle with caution. I try my best as a geographer not to romanticize or oversimplify what happened in history, but the tendency to do the opposite is common practice. *National Geographic*, for instance, is apt to portray the Maya as an assortment of relics, timeless throwbacks to a golden age before the Spanish conquest. Marxist texts cultivate another image, one in which the Maya emerge as inert victims forged and preserved by colonial exploitation. Neither representation fits satisfactorily what we now know to have been a variable experience, for the confrontation in Guatemala between natives and newcomers was something that differed quite markedly from region to region, if not from place to place within a region. If we view Mayas as subjects and not as objects, if we look at the particulars of the historical record and do not make do with myths and stereotypes, we can see them instead as social actors, as human agents who respond to invasion and domination in order to shape, at least in part, key elements of their culture. Viewing Mayas in this light, I believe, allows a more active emphasis to be placed on depicting their fate under Spanish rule.

---

When, in 1524, Spaniards first arrived in Guatemala, they found themselves in a difficult situation: wars of conquest would have to be waged not against a cohesive, hierarchical state, as had been the case in Mexico, but against quarrelsome, disparate polities long accustomed to harbouring grudge and grievance amongst themselves. Under these circumstances, conquest would be neither sudden nor sure.

It began with an incursion led by Pedro de Alvarado, whose forces entered Guatemala from Mexico three years after the fall of the Aztec capital, Tenochtitlán, to Hernán Cortés. The Spaniards encountered no appreciable Maya resistance along the Pacific coast, but following an ascent into the highlands a number of battles ensued. Alvarado's main opponents were the K'iche', but after their defeat other Maya peoples had to be dealt with, one by one by one—the Mam, the Ixil, and the Ch'orti' only three among many. On several occasions Kaqchikel warriors fought alongside the Spaniards, as in the conquest of the Tz'utujiles of Atitlán. Kaqchikel allegiance, however, withered after barely six months, when excessive demands for tribute caused them to stage a rebellion that lasted almost four years. Indian scribes wrote down their version of events in an account known as the *Annals of the Cakchiquels*:

> Ten days after we fled from the city [Yximché], Tunatiuh [Alvarado] began to make war upon us. On the day 4 Camey [September 5, 1524] they began to make us suffer. We scattered ourselves under the trees, under the vines. . . . All our tribes joined in the fight against Tunatiuh. The Spaniards began to leave at once. They went out of the city, leaving it deserted.
>
> Then the Cakchiquels began hostilities against the Spaniards. They dug holes and pits for the horses and scattered sharp stakes so that they should be killed. At the same time the people made war on them. Many Spaniards perished and the horses also. . . . Only thus did the Spaniards give them a breathing spell, [only thus] our hearts had some rest.
>
> On the day 1 Caok [March 27, 1527] our slaughter by the Spaniards began. The people fought them, and they continued to fight a prolonged war. Death struck us anew, but none of the people paid the tribute.

Some Mayas, the Q'eqchi's and the Uspantekos among them, inflicted temporary defeat on the invaders before succumbing to later, better organized acts of aggression. In one meandering foray, Pedro de Portocarrero, responsible for Spanish gains against the Kaqchikeles in 1527, pushed west across Guatemala and on into Chiapas, where he met up with fellow conquistador Diego de Mazariegos. This meeting most likely occurred in 1528, by which time Mazariegos may have got the better of Maya groups in Chiapas while the followers of Alvarado were still hard pressed in Guatemala. Not until some ten years later, in certain areas even longer, did Spaniards bring Maya groups in Guatemala to heel. Their resistance made the task of subjugation a savage, protracted affair.

The ability of Maya peoples to raise armies large enough to thwart Spanish ambitions is an important indication that Guatemala supported sizeable, well-organized populations when the Spaniards first invaded. One of my primary research interests is in the field of historical demography. A colleague and myself reckon that two million Mayas inhabited Guatemala on the eve of conquest, a number that fell precipitously to 428,000 by 1550, 236,500 by 1575, and 133,500 by 1595, before reaching a nadir level of 128,000 by 1625.

Population collapse can be attributed to many factors; foremost of all, however, is the role of disease. As with other Native American peoples, the Maya had no natural immunity to Old World maladies such as smallpox, measles, mumps, and plague, diseases which entered a "virgin soil" environment along with the invaders, with disastrous consequences for Indian welfare. Between 1519 and 1632 eight epidemics lashed Guatemala, with more localized episodes occurring over the same period. Quite often bouts of sickness triggered other crisis scenarios, for poor health resulted in failure to plant fields, which in turn led to food scarcity and the onset of famine. Once again, the Kaqchikel furnish us with a vivid eyewitness account, which tells of disease actually preceding the arrival of Alvarado by three or four years:

> It happened that during the twenty-fifth year [August 1519-October 1520] the plague began, oh, my sons! First they became ill of a cough, They suffered from nosebleeds and illness of the bladder. It was truly terrible, the number of dead there were in that period. The prince Vakaki Ahmak died then. Little by little heavy shadows and black night enveloped our fathers and grandfathers and us also, oh, my sons! When the plague raged.
>
> It was in truth terrible, the number of dead among the people. The people could not in any way control the sickness.
>
> Great was the stench of the dead. After our fathers and grandfathers succumbed, half of the people fled to the fields. The dogs and the vultures devoured the bodies. The mortality was terrible. Your grandfathers died, and with them died the son of the king and his brothers and kinsmen. So it was that we became orphans, oh, my sons! So we became when we were young. All of us were thus. We were born to die!

The immediate results of Spanish intrusion, then, were warfare, outbreaks of disease, and the beginning of native depopulation. After the trauma of these disruptions came the onerous responsibility of being Maya in the Spanish scheme of empire, a status that demanded expressions of loyalty and terms of commitment far different from those adhered to before. The Spaniards introduced various institutions to implement and meet their imperial expectations. Two institutions that figured prominently in the apparatus of conquest were *encomienda* and *congregación*.

The history of *encomienda* is complex, but throughout the sixteenth and seventeenth centuries it remained a device whereby privileged Spaniards or their Creole offspring received tribute in labour, goods, or cash from Indians entrusted to their charge. *Encomiendas* were not grants of land but, rather, awards to enjoy the fruits of what the land and its people could provide, whether prized items such as gold, silver, salt, or cacao or less spectacular produce such as corn, cloth, or chickens. The entitlement carried with it certain obligations, among them arranging that Indians held in *encomienda* received proper instruction in the tenets and practice of Christian faith, an obligation with which few Spaniards ever complied.

Grants of *encomienda* made shortly after conquest, assigned primarily to high-ranking officers who had fought for the Crown with distinction, frequently entailed the allocation of impressive amounts of tribute. *Encomenderos*, individuals who held and shared *encomiendas*, wielded considerable power early on as recipients of Indian tribute, but the Crown's role with respect to *encomienda* was one of diplomatic curtailment. It eventually took measures to dismantle privileges—placing restrictions on labour provisions and limiting inheritance beyond one or two generations—so that even the most enterprising of *encomenderos* would be stopped from becoming the equivalent of a feudal lord. Of particular importance in this regard were reforms carried out between 1548 and 1555, when Alonso López de Cerrato served as president of the Audiencia de Guatemala, a court whose members were appointed by the Crown and charged with the day-to-day government of far-flung territory from Chiapas to Costa Rica. When it was abolished in the eighteenth century, *encomienda* represented little more than a modest form of pension.

*Encomiendas* encompassed, in varying spatial degree, one or more communities that Spaniards referred to as *pueblos de indios*, Indian towns in the municipal sense of central place and surrounding countryside, segregated areas where non-Indians in theory were not supposed to settle. Upon arrival Spaniards observed that Maya settlements were customarily more dispersed than nucleated. What little urbanization that had developed was restricted to defensive, hilltop sites not in the least conducive to proper and efficient administration.

The policy of *congregación* was designed to deal with this anarchy, and *pueblos de indios* were the result of its zealous implementation.

As promulgated by Spanish law, *congregación* was a means whereby Mayas found dwelling in scattered rural groups would be brought together, converted to Christianity, and moulded into harmonious, resourceful communities that reflected imperial notions of orderly, civilized life. To the Church, especially members of the Dominican and Franciscan orders, fell the difficult job of getting Indian families down from the mountains and resettled in towns built around a Catholic place of worship. A royal order issued on March 21, 1551, spells out the mandate to missionize, and the rationalization behind it:

> With great care and particular attention we have always attempted to impose the most convenient means of instructing the Indians in the Holy Catholic Faith and evangelical law, causing them to forget their ancient erroneous rites and ceremonies and to live in concert and order; and, so that this might be brought about, those of our Council of [the] Indies have met together several times with other religious persons . . . and they, with the desire of promoting the service of God, and ours, resolved that the Indians should be reduced to villages and not be allowed to live divided and separated in the mountains and wildernesses, where they are deprived of all spiritual and temporal comforts, the aid of our ministers, and those other things which human necessities oblige men to give one to another; therefore . . . the viceroys, presidents, and governors [are] charged and ordered to execute the reduction, settlement, and indoctrination of the Indians.

The rhetoric of *congregación* belongs to what Carlos Fuentes has called the "legal country," a colonial fiction distinctly at variance with the "real country" that came into being. In the overall vision of empire, few endeavours differed in outcome so markedly from original intent as did *congregación*, prompting contemporary observers to express outrage, astonishment, and despair that such a grand plan could amount to so little. *Congregación* did make its mark on the landscape at an early date: *pueblos de indios* created by regular and secular clergy in the course of the sixteenth century persist today as *municipios*, or townships, that generations of anthropologists have considered the key unit in defining Maya community life. But no sooner had Spaniards resettled Indians where the Crown deemed suitable than did the Maya drift back to the mountains that they and their families had been moved from. Why did this happen? What caused the grip of *congregación* to become undone?

For one thing, *congregación* was carried out not by persuasion but by force. Because entire families were shifted against their will from one location to another, it was unlikely that people who found the experience disagreeable, if not hateful, would stay put. Mayas repeatedly fled to outlying rural areas to escape the exploitation they suffered while resident in town or nearby. There they could be free of compulsory demands to furnish tribute, provide labour, work on local roads or the parish church, and serve as human carriers. They also sought the refuge of the mountains when disease struck, the occurrence of illness in, and its impact on, *pueblos de indios* correctly perceived as being more destructive than arms-length subsistence in the hills. Furthermore, how the Maya farmed the highlands was usually best undertaken by living not in large, agglomerated centres but in small, dispersed groups.

There is next the issue of denominational friction and the deployment of spiritual resources. Along with the Mercedarians, a less-dominant third party in the missionary enterprise, Dominicans and Franciscans waged a territorial war while being simultaneously driven by the higher calling of *congregación*. The two largest, most powerful orders each carved out a sphere of influence relative to the colonial capital of Santiago de Guatemala. Dominicans moved into the far north and west, responsible for a vast, daunting expanse that stretched from Verapaz to Chiapas. Franciscans opted for a more manageable central zone within a fifty-kilometre radius of Lake Atitlán. Both orders jealously guarded against rival encroachment the *pueblos de indios* established in the confines of their jurisdictions. Bickering between them diverted energy from the pressing concern of native conversion and became so tiresome that the Crown issued a royal order on January 22, 1556, commanding the friars, accused of "petty ambition" and "name calling," to resolve their differences and conduct themselves in a more seemly, Christian fashion.

Such behaviour, in the eyes of the Crown, set a bad example and made little practical sense, given that friars were few and their responsibilities many. Indeed, throughout the colonial period less than one thousand missionaries arrived in Guatemala to propagate the faith. Civil authorities well recognized the uphill battle that their religious associates faced; two Crown officers, Antonio Rodríguez de Quesada and Pedro Ramírez de Quiñones, openly acknowledged that "in these parts there is a great lack of missionaries." By the mid-sixteenth century the Dominicans were so overextended that they ceded a large part of their beat to the Mercedarians, a more acceptable choice to the Dominicans than their Franciscan adversaries. For their part, as early as 1552 the Franciscans requested permission from the Crown to assume responsibility for establishing missions in Dominican territory, "because the fathers of Santo Domingo are just not up to it."

At the other end of the Maya realm, to the south and east of Santiago, none of the three orders established a notable presence, leaving the Oriente in the proselytizing hands of the less-experienced secular clergy. The divide in missionary jurisdiction between a "secular" east and a "regular" west is an important one to recognize. Ecclesiastical divisions, however, serve only to underscore another more profound process, one best articulated by Murdo MacLeod in his landmark work on the colonial experience in Central America.

MacLeod argues that exploitation of the isthmian resource base operated in such a way that Spanish attention focused either on the cacao-rich Pacific coast or on the rolling, temperate lands to the south and east of the capital, where indigo could be grown, cattle grazed, and two or even three corn crops harvested each year. The Spaniards viewed the *tierra fría*, or cold land, to the north and west of Santiago—more difficult of access and with fewer entrepreneurial options—as far less attractive. Their interest in the north and west, therefore, was never as intense as their interest in the south and east. When Spanish attitudes concerning the worth of the land were translated into thousands of individual actions, they resulted in a notably different colonial experience.

South and east of Santiago de Guatemala, the Spaniards encroached upon Maya communities to a greater degree, and cultural and biological assimilation proceeded at a brisker pace. There, as in El Salvador, Honduras, and Nicaragua, Spaniards and Africans mixed with Indians to create a predominantly *mestizo* or Ladino milieu. To the north and west of the capital, where possibilities for enrichment were less and fewer Spaniards were inclined to settle, Maya peoples withstood the onslaught of acculturation more resiliently, holding on to much of their land, retaining traditional principles of community organization, and guarding a sense of identity that was resolutely their own. Maya languages were kept alive, as were Maya ways of worshipping the gods. Daily chores and the seasonal round followed a Maya, not a Spanish, rhythm. Even time itself, the days and months that make up a year, ticked on with a Maya pulse. When, existentially, *congregación* is situated within this larger panorama, Maya reaction to it takes on a vital, formative dynamic.

Condemned by geography to inhabit a backwater region in the Spanish scheme of empire, the Maya of Guatemala shaped for themselves a culture of refuge in which Hispanic traits and institutions were absorbed and mixed with indigenous ones, often in elaborate ways that baffled, mocked, and in the end eroded imperial authority. Periodization is somewhat difficult. Certainly by the seventeenth century, patterns of hybrid mores were much in evidence, but the trend had set in earlier. Recognition that all was far from well, that *congregación* was not unfolding according to plan, prompted the following remarks by Pedro Ramírez de Quiñones, uttered in frustration on May 20, 1556:

> There is great disorder among the Indians in matters that relate to their government and administration. Things are chaotic, lacking direction. Grave public sins abound. What is most of concern is that Indian actions go unpunished, without redress, because they are not brought to the attention of the court. In most *pueblos de indios* people live much as they wish to, or can, and since the court cannot arrange for visitations to be made, we, its officers, cannot vouch for one-tenth of the district we are in charge of.

Even when Indians displaced by *congregación* chose to remain within its spatial embrace, they frequently regrouped in town or close by along pre-conquest domestic lines that Spaniards called *parcialidades*. These were social units of great antiquity, organized as patrilineal clans or localized kin affiliates, and usually associated with particular tracts of land.

Unfamiliarity on the part of missionaries as to the discrete nature of *parcialidades* often resulted in several of them being thrown together to form, in theory, a single Indian community. Once gathered around a new centre, however, *parcialidades* would preserve their aboriginal identity by continuing to operate socially and economically as separate components rather than merging to form a corporate body. Far from being the placid, homogeneous entities that colonial legislation conjures up, many *pueblos de indios* turned out to be a mosaic of *parcialidades* that touched but did not interpenetrate, that co-existed but did not always co-operate. In the Province of Totonicapán, for instance, nine *pueblos de indios* alone comprised over thirty *parcialidades*, each of them assessed individually for tribute-paying purposes in the late seventeenth century. At least one of these towns, Sacapulas, also arranged that land be held and farmed by *parcialidad*, as did other *pueblos de indios*. *Parcialidades* might too be associated with specific *cofradías*, religious sodalities originally introduced for the worship of a favoured saint but which, over time, came to serve as useful Christian cover for more suspect forms of worship.

---

If residential commitment to *congregación* resulted in a certain degree of improvisation, town abandonment led to manifest aberrations. The rot, once again, set in early. Sacapulas, for example, may not have crystallized quite as its Dominican founders first imagined, but once their convent had been established a well-defined community did form around it. Another matter entirely was the outlying countryside.

Archival work can be a tedious, monotonous grind, a ritual of days spent sifting through documents for marginal, inconsequential returns. Occasionally something out of the ordinary turns up, like the letter I found in the Archive of the Indies in Seville that deals "hands-on" with conducting God's work among the Maya of Sacapulas.

The letter was penned in the convent at Sacapulas on December 6, 1555, by Tomás de Cárdenas and Juan de Torres, who wrote to King Charles V, Holy Roman Emperor, about the tremendous obstacles working against effective *congregación*. They mention, first, the difficulties imposed by the environment, stating not unreasonably that "this part of the sierra is the most rugged and broken to be found in these lands." Making their way across it, Cárdenas and

Torres had stumbled upon groups "of eight, six, and even four houses or huts, tucked and hidden away in gullies where, until the arrival of one of us, no other Spaniard had reached." The friars lament that during their trek they discovered "idols in abundance, not just concealed but placed in people's houses more or less as they had had them before they were baptized."

Indians, they tell the King, populate such desolate, faraway places so that "no-one could reach there who might disturb or destroy their evil living." The people they had found living that way, the Dominicans state with some relief, "now that they are housed together will have less opportunity to practise idolatry and, ourselves, more opportunity to watch over them." Thus resettled, Indians "can more readily be instructed not only in matters that concern our Holy Faith but also in proper human conduct."

To those who might bemoan that *congregación* is carried out involuntarily, that it shifts families from one place to another against their will, Cárdenas and Torres boldly declare that "there is no sick person who does not find the taste of medicine unpleasant." In this sense Indians are held to be "like children," and so "one must do not what most pleases them but what is best for them."

If, at times, the tone of the friars is sober and paternalistic, so also is it poignant and insightful. Nowhere do the Dominicans capture more perceptively why Maya families might resist and resent resettlement than when they remark: "Among all these Indians there is not one who wishes to leave behind the hut passed on to him by his father, nor to abandon a pestilential ravine or desert some inaccessible craggy rocks, for that is where the bones of his forefathers rest."

Solemn words, but voiced with a sense of foreboding that soon proved well-founded. Five years after Cárdenas and Torres addressed the Crown, the native leaders of Santiago Atítlán also wrote to complain that in outlying settlements they were responsible for there lived "rebellious Indians who wish to remain outside our authority and who disobey our orders concerning what tribute should be paid." Even near the capital city desertion was rife; the years between 1575 and 1578 witnessed "many Indians" in the environs of Santiago "moving about, in hiding, from one place to another" rather than be forced to furnish their own tribute as well as pay that part deemed still to be owed by deceased relatives. Around this same time, farther north in the Verapaz, it was reported that "*parcialidades* and entire families leave to live idolatrously in the mountains." Two sizeable *pueblos de indios*, Santa Catalina and Zulbén, had been abandoned almost completely by 1579, only five years after the Bishop of Verapaz himself had supervised the process of *congregación*. At Santa María Cahabón, baptized Mayas allegedly gave up civilized life to join unconquered Lacandón and Chol-Manché tribes in pre-Christian barbarism on the other side of the frontier.

A century or so later, after the Bishop of Guatemala, Andrés de las Navas, had twice toured his jurisdiction and heard disturbing reports from parish priests about fugitivism, lawlessness, idolatry, and tax evasion, he prepared a dossier that leaves little doubt about how widespread "civil disobedience" had become. Outside San Juan Sacatepéquez, at a place called Pajuiú, Indians "who neither hear mass nor confess their sins" had lived "for upwards of twenty years, dwelling there under the pretext of growing corn." Other centrally located *pueblos de indios*—Chimaltenango, Parramos, Patzicía, Patzún, San Andrés Itzapa, San Martín Jilotepeque, Sumpango, and Tecpán among them—also drew the bishop's wrath. Religious backsliding was only one element of waywardness that concerned him. At Comalapa the parish priest told of "daykeepers and witchdoctors," informing Las Navas, "After we preach to them, warning them that they must cease their ancient superstitions, they leave church and are heard to ask: 'Why should we abandon the ways of our grandfathers and ancestors?'"

Such attitudes among Indians living reasonably close to Santiago were, if anything, magnified farther away from the capital, nowhere more blatantly than at San Mateo Ixtatán. There, high up in the Sierra de los Cuchumatanes, Fray Alonso de León records that he had recently been informed "that some eighty families do not figure on the tribute list," which meant not only that "His Majesty is losing revenue" but also that "all these fugitives do not attend mass or go to confession." The relationship between father and son, the priest declared, was one in which "nothing is passed on save for how to take care of the cornfields and how to live all day long like savages in the hills. De León feared that proper codes of behaviour would never take root, for the people of San Mateo "are at each other's throats, all year long."

What distressed Fray Alonso most was that Indians had decided "to build a shrine, on no authority but their own, up in the hills some distance from town, at precisely the same spot where the sacrificial altar of pagan times used to be." The shrine was located "on a hill top, between the remains of ancient temples, which they call *cues*, where on any given day may be found charcoal and incense and other signs of burnt offerings." De León disclosed that "further transgressions against Holy Church include the sacrifice of turkeys, taken up to the hills to be dispatched with the blood of other animals." Each March, at a place two leagues distant from town, wood was piled at the foot of crosses that were later set on fire. The *"indios diabólicos"* of San Mateo, it was alleged, "with their nasty habits and evil deeds have contaminated the entire town in such a way that it remains Christian in name only."

Life in the "real country," then, jarred dramatically with the blueprint legislated in the "legal country." It would be a mistake to imagine, however, that even though the Maya made unworthy converts, nothing could be gained from exploiting them, that Spaniards somehow were disposed to shrugging off their quest for power and enrichment so easily. Officials of both the Church and the Crown from time to time did very well at native expense, legally or otherwise.

In terms of illegality, perhaps the most obnoxious demand placed on native communities came in the form of *repartimientos*. Under this practice, *corregidores* and *alcaldes mayores*, district governors who actually bought public office with a view to making money from it, supplied Indians with various commodities, insisting that they be purchased at prices favourable to the seller, regardless of whether or not the recipients desired the merchandise in the first place. A reverse strategy was to force a sale at rock-bottom prices in one area, then re-sell at higher prices in another.

*Repartimientos* appear on the scene in the sixteenth century, and feature in the seventeenth also, although they seem to have been most prolific in the eighteenth century. One item that figured prominently in these dealings was cotton, which district governors distributed in raw, bulk form among Mayan women, compelling them to spin it into thread and then weave it into lengths of cloth, or *mantas*. The finished article fetched a tidy profit—for the *corregidor* or *alcalde mayor*, not the worker—when sold at market. Raw wool was also circulated, among male weavers, with the same end in mind. Other items peddled to the Indians included axes, clothes, hats, iron tools and implements, mules, and (on occasion) money. Although native leaders petitioned against these transactions, stating that *repartimientos* caused parents to neglect their families and to slight their fields, directives ordering government officials to cease their odious racket were repeatedly ignored.

Just as Indians were vulnerable to exploitation by government officials, so also did they fall prey to exactions by the clergy. An order issued as early as 1561 stipulated what goods and services priests could legitimately request from their parishioners. Theoretical limits, however, were not always adhered to, and so while many Spaniards did work selflessly among the Maya, others concerned themselves more with personal gain than with indigenous salvation. Abuses again seem to have been especially prevalent in the eighteenth century, with priests and friars accused of various excesses, including failure to reimburse for personal services, selling livestock without the owner's consent, overzealous collection of funds to celebrate mass or to hear confession, and embezzlement of *cofradía* assets.

Three centuries of colonial rule cast a long and oppressive shadow, creating deep and enduring fissures in the nature of Guatemalan social, economic, and political life. Certainly by the time of independence, which took place in 1821, little had changed (or was about to) in the fundamental way that Spaniards from all walks of life treated and related to Indians. For them, as for Creoles and Ladinos also, Maya subordination was not an issue of polemic or debate: it was simply taken for granted, something that was regarded as a natural right, an unqueried fixture in the imperial enterprise. Co-existence under these terms fostered neither compassion nor respect. What it *did* breed were mutual feelings of suspicion, distrust, hatred, and fear.

In comprehending how subordination was maintained, anthropologist Michael Taussig offers some trenchant remarks. "We would be most unwise," he cautions, "to overlook or underestimate the role of terror." Terror, asserts Taussig, is not only "a physiological state" but also "a social fact and a cultural construction whose baroque dimensions allow it to serve as the mediator *par excellence* of colonial hegemony." Like many features created by Spanish conquest, the spectre of terror—pervading "spaces of death" in which "Indian, African, and White gave birth to the New World"— haunted Maya life to scar and disfigure succeeding centuries.

# CHAPTER EIGHTEEN

# *The Century after Independence*

I FIND IT IRONIC to think that we often know more about the history of Guatemala under Spanish rule than we do about post-colonial times, especially the nineteenth century. Bit by bit, however, a more grounded appreciation of the events and circumstances of nineteenth-century life is emerging. Much of the credit for this belongs to a historian at Tulane University, Ralph Lee Woodward, Jr. His research, while focusing primarily on the political career of Rafael Carrera, in effect sketches the lineaments of culture and society during the first half-century of Guatemala's existence as an independent republic. The years between 1821 and 1871 have also attracted the attention of another distinguished historian, E. Bradford Burns.

What Burns and Woodward tell us about the conditions of rural life in Guatemala contrasts vividly with portrayals of what took place in the countryside after 1871, when the rule of Liberal not Conservative governments prevailed. Our knowledge of rural life from 1871 on has been advanced considerably by the findings of several scholars, among them Shelton Davis, David McCreery, David Stoll, and John Watanabe. The research of these individuals affords us a glimpse of the changes that occurred in Guatemala during the century after independence. Contemplation of historical forces operating at the national or regional level can be fleshed out by more detailed scrutiny of the impact they had in distinct local settings. Of particular interest to me are the communities of Santiago Chimaltenango,

Nebaj, Santa Eulalia, and San Juan Ixcoy, all four of which are Maya strongholds in the Sierra de los Cuchumatanes, the area of Guatemala I perhaps know best.

---

The political scene in Guatemala following independence from Spain was marked by prolonged internal conflict between Conservatives and Liberals for control of government office. Differences between the two camps were many, but centred around a Conservative preference for maintaining Hispanic-derived institutions that sought to preserve the colonial status quo, in contrast to a Liberal preference for creating an entirely new social and economic order that viewed progress as attainable by promoting capitalist links with the outside world. In terms of the impact of ideology on Maya ways, Conservatism represented a continuation of the culture of refuge shaped during colonial times. Liberalism signified Maya assimilation into a modern, outward-looking Ladino state. Conservatism meant minimal cultural change at the community level, Liberalism intense, outside interference that would alter irrevocably long-established ways of living with the land.

Liberals dominated political office between 1823 and 1839, but their plans for radical reform were stalled if not reversed for three decades thereafter when Rafael Carrera led the Conservatives to power following a popular uprising. A wily, pragmatic individual who came to be known as "protector of the people," Carrera undid the work of his Liberal predecessor, Mariano Gálvez, and championed a stable, paternalist state founded on restored Hispanic institutions. The extent to which Maya communities benefited directly from Carrera's political agenda is unclear. Although Woodward (1990) maintains that "Carrera's pro-Indian policy did indeed protect the Indians from further encroachment on their land and labor during the 1840s," he concedes that "after 1850 that protection began to lessen as Carrera became more clearly attached to the Guatemalan elite." McCreery is more convinced by the reasoning of the late Oliver La Farge (1940), who suggested some time ago that Maya life under Carrera "becomes a smooth blend; well stabilized, it has the individuality and roundness that mark any culture, and its continued evolution is in the form of growth out of itself, rather than in response to alien pressures." McCreery (1990) argues that his research findings tend to support the views of La Farge. He depicts Carrera's program as one in which a "fragile and beleaguered state issued laws and decrees but could visit little effective attention on a rural population that resisted paying taxes and for whose land and labor the ladino elites had little use." Maya communities, McCreery concludes, were "more neglected than protected" by Carrera, a claim that diminishes or makes less relevant the role of the state in Indian life.

Liberals regained political office in 1871, six years after Carrera's death, and under the stewardship of Justo Rufino Barrios began to implement with fervour what they had been frustrated from doing four decades earlier. Burns (1980) describes the Liberal agenda as signalling "a return to monoculture, declining food production for local consumption, rising foreign debt, forced labor, debt peonage, the growth of latifundia, and the greater impoverishment of the majority." Attacks on Maya land and assaults on Maya labour were inevitable consequences of the Liberal vision of progress.

McCreery argues that Barrios and his successors did not entirely eradicate the notion of community property. What Liberal legislation demanded was for land to be formally declared and, if possible, registered not by collective but by individual title. The option of registering land communally was not ruled out; it was simply more acceptable—the preferred, ideologically correct choice—to register land as individual property. McCreery (1988) makes a crucial point: "Because the process of conversion to private property rested on a number of individual, positive acts, it progressed at very different rates from village to village, depending on external conditions and on the dictates of community traditions and circumstances." While "positive acts" on the part of Maya communities by no means guaranteed lawful title to land, failure to lay claim to title exposed them to risks of seizure and encroachment.

Land was most certainly lost; exactly how much has yet to be ascertained. Scholarly opinion ranges from Robert Naylor's vague impression (1967) of there being "little discernible change" in Maya life, of its continuing "much the same as before," to Carol Smith's more realistic but undocumented assertion (1984) that Maya communities "lost about half of the lands they traditionally claimed during the colonial period." More systematic research is clearly in order.

Land was transformed from a cultural into an economic resource, from community to commodity, by Liberal desires to capitalize on Guatemala's untapped potential as a producer of coffee. The Pacific piedmont and the Verapaz highlands in particular offered ideal growing conditions. Both these regions had been relatively untouched by the search for a successful cash crop during colonial times, which had seen cacao, cochineal, and indigo enjoy short-lived cycles of boom and bust. Investment by domestic and foreign capital resulted in coffee emerging during the second half of the nineteenth century as Guatemala's principal export crop, a position it has maintained in the national economy from the time of President Barrios until today. Organized on a *finca* or plantation basis, coffee production demands intensive labour input, mostly at harvest time. What suits the requirements of coffee planters best, therefore, is a seasonal workforce, one that provides labour when needed and that can be dispensed with when not. Outright coercion in the form of a draft known as *mandamiento*, authorized by President Barrios in 1876, reinforced the long-standing practice of legalized debt peonage, which endured well into the twentieth century in Guatemala, when it was eventually replaced by a vagrancy law requiring individuals holding less than a stipulated amount of land to work part of each year as wage labourers for others: anyone farming ten or more *cuerdas*, but less than the three or four *manzanas* that qualified them for an exemption, was expected to work one hundred days; anyone farming less than ten *cuerdas* was expected to work one hundred and fifty days.★ A *libreta*, or identification book, had to be carried at all times and was best inspected with the requisite number of work days fulfilled.

With the advent of Liberal rule, then, Maya communities throughout Guatemala were exposed to a double threat, one that targeted labour as well as land as desirable economic assets. The degree to which Liberal prerogatives made their mark on Indian life, however, varied considerably from community to community, as the following case studies amply demonstrate.

---

★ A *cuerda* is a variable unit of land, measuring either 0.11 acres or 0.27 acres. A *manzana* equals approximately 1.7 acres.

## Santiago Chimaltenango

Santiago Chimaltenango, known to local residents simply as Chimbal, is a Mam community lying along the southern flanks of the Sierra de los Cuchumatanes at elevations ranging from around 1,400 to over 2,700 metres. While growing conditions in lower-elevation *tierra templada* are favourable, the cultivation of coffee as a cash crop in Chimbal dates only to the middle of the twentieth century, primarily as an activity of small-scale producers. Chimbal was studied in the 1930s by Charles Wagley, who produced two benchmark accounts (1941, 1949). Forty years after Wagley first visited, Chimbal attracted the attention of another anthropologist, John Watanabe, whose work provides insight into land-related incidents in the late nineteenth century.

Chimbal is an interesting case. In terms of the overall impact of the Liberal reforms, it cannot be said to have suffered the worst of transformations. What Chimbal's experience illustrates, however, is that moves to lay claim to title triggered counterclaims on the part of neighbouring communities, often with detrimental consequences.

Watanabe informs us that on May 19, 1879, representatives from Chimbal lodged a petition with the district governor of Huehuetenango for legal title to community land. Chimbal's petition was submitted two years after the Barrios administration issued Decree 170, which terminated the colonial system of land rental known as *censo enfiteusis*. Under *censo enfiteusis*, community residents could acquire usufruct rights to specific plots of land, rights that could be inherited, sold, sublet, or exchanged but did not allow for the legal transfer of land itself. These were precisely the arrangements Decree 170 was designed to eliminate.

Chimbal's petition provoked a contrary response from three of its neighbours, all of them alleging that tracts of the land claimed by Chimbal belonged to them. San Juan Atitán was first to protest, stating on June 20, 1879, that six years previously it had claimed lands included in the Chimbal petition. San Pedro Necta followed, stating in November that a village called Niyá fell within its territory, not Chimbal's. San Martín Cuchumatán declared jurisdiction over a village called Tajumuc, which it said it had incorporated long before. Chimbal, in turn, disputed all three counterclaims, and in December it requested that a survey be arranged to resolve the matter.

Responsibility for the survey fell to one Juan María Ordóñez, who was charged with measuring land designated as *ejido*, a standard allotment of one square league (16.6 square kilometres) around the main township centre, and *baldío*, an indeterminate amount of public or state land beyond. Ordóñez conducted the survey between June 2 and June 17, 1880, and subsequently filed a report that calculated Chimbal's *ejido* to be 17.4 square kilometres in extent, surrounded by almost 54 square kilometres of *baldío*. The land disputed with San Pedro and San Martín—San Juan, by now, had apparently withdrawn from the fray—lay exclusively in the *baldío*. Three years later a government official reviewing Ordóñez's report observed that Chimbal enjoyed access to more *ejido* land than its old colonial entitlement. He also noted that *baldío* land contested by San Pedro totalled almost 25 square kilometres. When a municipal title was finally issued on September 10, 1891, it recognized as *ejido* all 17.4 square kilometres registered in Ordóñez's survey but awarded to Chimbal little more than half the land, some 29 square kilometres, claimed as *baldío*.

Out of a total claim of 71 square kilometres, then, Chimbal ended up with legal title to 46. The 25 square kilometres forfeited in the dispute, Watanabe reckons, went in equal measure to San Pedro and San Martín, with the latter's share being absorbed by Todos Santos Cuchumatán when San Martín became part of its municipal jurisdiction.

The stakes at Chimbal, compared to what was up for grabs elsewhere in Guatemala, may have been slim, but the titling episode is instructive on three counts. First, by pitting neighbour against neighbour, Maya against Maya, the practice conformed to that most obdurate rule of conquest: divide and rule. Second, it established that a new order would indeed replace the old, for land henceforth would be owned, not merely worked. And three, it represented the beginnings of Maya accommodation to the modern Ladino state, which Watanabe (1992) expresses thus: "In seeking legal title— whether municipal or individual—to safeguard their lands, Chimaltecos in effect abdicated sovereignty over that land by appealing to state authority to validate their claims." Further accommodation would be necessary as the power of the state grew.

## Nebaj

Nebaj, one of three Ixil townships lying at the eastern edge of the Cuchumatanes mountains, embraces municipal territory ranging from below 1,400 to upwards of 3,000 metres in elevation. Nebaj and its two Ixil neighbours, Chajul and San Juan Cotzal, were studied in the early 1940s by Jackson Steward Lincoln. His untimely death while engaged in fieldwork in Guatemala cut short a promising career, if Lincoln's posthumously published notes (1945) are anything to judge by. Benjamin Colby and Pierre van den Berghe (1969), whose research activities in the 1960s focused on ethnic relations, also subjected all three Ixil townships to rewarding scrutiny. Ixil country was hard hit by the counterinsurgency war of the early 1980s, in the wake of which David Stoll (1993) conducted a detailed examination of the community life of people who, in the words of several survivors, had been caught "between two fires." Stoll's work on the nineteenth and early twentieth centuries draws in part on archival investigation by Elaine Elliott.

Colby and van den Berghe, as well as Stoll, lean heavily on Lincoln in depicting how the coffee economy "opened-up" Ixil country. Labour, not land, appears initially to have been the big attraction. The prospect of recruiting seasonal workers lured to Nebaj one Isaías Palacios, a Spaniard who arrived in the early 1890s to take up the post of town secretary. He soon became Nebaj's first labour contractor, forwarding loans in return for commitments to work on coffee plantations. Palacios and agents like him sealed contracts with the assistance of drink, proffering Indians liquor, trapping them into debt and dependency, and cultivating a pattern of behaviour from which escape was difficult. Stoll invokes the words of the Irish-Canadian archaeologist Robert Burkitt, who in 1913, while staying at Nebaj, observed "an unceasing coming and going of labor contractors and plantation agents getting out gangs of Indians for the Pacific Coast." Burkitt (1930) pulled no punches and spoke frankly about what he saw:

> Years ago, when I first visited Nebaj, it was a different place from now.... I had struck the place at an especially bad moment. The plantation agents were at the height of their activity, scattering money, advance pay for work, and every Indian was able to

buy rum. The rum business and the coffee business work together in this country, automatically. The plantation advances money to the Indian and the rum seller takes it away from him and the Indian has to go to work again. Work leads to rum and rum leads to work. . . . I used to think that Chichicastenango was the drunkenest town in the country, but now I think it is Nebaj. My plans at Nebaj were upset by rum. There are two ruin places that I know of that are to be got at from Nebaj and I did nothing at either of them, and one of them I never even saw. The Indians I was going to take were never sober.

Lincoln also noted connections between the "rum business" and the "coffee business," acknowledging that while "Indians drank on all ceremonial occasions" it was Ladinos who were responsible "for increasing the amount and the strength of the liquor for the purpose of enriching themselves." Nebaj at one juncture supported eighty watering holes, which lends some credibility to Burkitt's claim that Indians there were "drunk from morning to night." Stoll attributes a key role to Ladinos who moved to Nebaj from Malacatán, now Malacatancito, a town near Huehuetenango. These people and other Ladinos, Stoll claims, by "selling liquor and loaning the cash needed to go on binges . . . separated Ixils from much of their best arable land," for after an agreement was struck "anything less than prompt repayment meant that the house or land put up for collateral could change hands."

To land lost in this manner was added further amounts appropriated during the titling process. When a municipal title for 388 *caballerías* was issued in 1885 to San Juan Cotzal, 180 *caballerías* also went to private individuals, a substantial amount of the total land available.* Chajul received title to 2,424 *caballerías* in 1900, an additional 157 *caballerías* being allocated to private individuals. Nebaj was awarded 1,237 *caballerías* in 1903, with 87 *caballerías* privately titled. Most of the land deeded to private individuals was in lower-lying *tierra templada* at elevations suitable for raising coffee or sugar cane.

Serious loss occurred in the far north of Ixil country, especially in Sotzil and Ilom, which retained little more than the land surrounding residential compounds. Chel, Ixtupil, and Sacsiguán did not for-

---

* A *caballería* of land measures about 112 acres or 45.4 hectares.

feit as much, but they did lose their most prized units of land. The claimant whose name kept appearing on title deeds was Lisandro Gordillo Galán, a Mexican citizen recorded in 1895 as having served as the town secretary of Chajul. Stoll observes: "Titling land may not seem the most obvious way to lose it, but such has been the experience of indigenous people, because what can be titled can be alienated." Irregularities in the way that land was owned and operated in Ixil country continued well into the twentieth century.

## Santa Eulalia

A Q'anjob'al community situated in the northern reaches of the Sierra de los Cuchumatanes, Santa Eulalia incorporates territory that stretches from *tierra caliente* around 800 metres in elevation to *tierra fría* well above the township centre at 2,600 metres. Oliver La Farge visited Santa Eulalia in 1932, and his study of an array of Maya cultural expressions there (1947) remains one of the landmark contributions in Mesoamerican anthropology. Another anthropologist, Shelton Davis, studied the community in the 1960s. His doctoral dissertation (1970) is a model of historically informed ethnography, certainly the best inquiry we have to date of how national-level politics shaped local-level landholding in Guatemala in the late nineteenth century.

Assessing the impact of the Barrios reforms was not the primary reason that La Farge or Davis studied Santa Eulalia. Neither of them, however, could address their research questions without looking into land and labour relations. What La Farge considered the "happy isolation" of the Cuchumatanes mountains "was shattered in the last half of the nineteenth century when the development of the coffee *fincas* on the Pacific slopes of the Sierra Madre produced a demand for labor which could be filled only by drawing upon the population reservoirs of the highlands." Labour may have been plentiful, but in the case of Santa Eulalia land itself was also a major consideration. The community estate traditionally encompassed fertile land at elevations ideal for raising coffee, which did not escape entrepreneurial curiosity. La Farge had earlier established the validity of Stoll's observation, recording that a "survey" of Santa Eulalia "resulted in the passing of much valuable land into the hands of Ladinos and a considerable reduction in the extent of the *ejidos*, or common lands." Not until Davis arrived on the scene was the magnitude of loss more fully discerned.

Davis begins by noting that, although the Laws of the Indies in colonial times and republican legislation under Carrera in theory protected Maya rights to communal land, in practice "they never clearly defined the actual limits of these Indian estates." Reluctance to do so was clearly a matter of exercising power, for "giving Indian *municipios* the legal right to ancient estates, especially those in the hot country areas distant from pueblo centers, meant that political control and ecclesiastical conversion would be impossible." Tenure arrangements that were "chaotic and unstructured" led to bitter disputes about land rights, which set one Maya community against another and allowed opportunistic intervention on the part of Ladino interests.

Davis reckons that, over the forty-year period covered by his data, roughly 70 per cent of Santa Eulalia's land fell into Ladino hands, including land in Barillas and the Ixcán, "zones of greatest ecological and economic potential." Of fifty-five lots titled in these areas, Indians received only nine; of the 1,520 *caballerías* involved in the titling process, Indians were awarded 183. Ladinos titled land, as the government wished, individually, not as a corporate body, the customary Maya way of laying claim. Titles issued to Ladinos were frequently in excess of thirty *caballerías*. As Ladinos carved up the *tierra caliente* in latifundia fashion, the Maya of Santa Eulalia concentrated on acquiring legal hold of the *tierra fría* around the town centre. A classic Latin American dichotomy emerged of large, Ladino-owned estates in the lowlands and a patchwork of small, Indian-tilled fields in the highlands.

Davis records that the first land lost was around the village of Santa Cruz Yalmux, where a group of Ladinos from Huehuetenango claimed some two hundred *caballerías*. The claimants, members of the local militia, made their case on May 22, 1888, appearing in person before General Manuel Lisandro Barillas, then president of Guatemala. They laid claim on the grounds that: (1) the *ejidos* of Santa Eulalia in *tierra fría* "were large and sufficient" for the Indians who lived there; (2) the petitioners would deploy the lands to which they sought title "for the development of capitalistic agriculture"; (3) during "the rise to power of Justo Rufino Barrios" Huehuetenango had played a "military role," which the government was obliged to recognize; and (4) issuing title to land would allow for the creation of a new *municipio*, which would function "as a military outpost for the protection of the frontier between Mexico and Guatemala" along the Usumacinta River. Despite protests that the claimants "only wished to gain title to this land so as to later resell it to Indian residents," the Barillas government awarded two hundred *caballerías* of Yalmux land to the Ladinos of Huehuetenango in July 1888. On October 17 that same year the *municipio* of Barillas came into being. The choice of place name directly linked government action with the erosion of the Maya estate.

Despite lobbying for land in order to stimulate "capitalistic agriculture," Ladinos who received title did not develop their property. What did develop was small-scale cattle ranching, with the new owners more commonly renting out land as absentee landlords to Indian occupants. Other Maya families, however, paid no formal rent and simply continued to subsist as "illegal squatters" on land that they still considered as belonging to them. Not until much later was the agricultural potential of the Ixcán systematically exploited, resulting in an inevitable clash of interests.

## San Juan Ixcoy

San Juan Ixcoy is a Q'anjob'al township located in the heart of the Cuchumatán highlands mostly in *tierra fría* upwards of 1,500 metres in elevation. The town centre lies at around 2,200 metres in a narrow valley drained by the San Juan River. San Juan has yet to receive the scholarly attention afforded other Maya communities. It is a gloomy, unwelcoming place that keeps outsiders at bay, as if the memory of the carnage that occurred there in 1898 still lingers, giving it a grim reputation even by the standards of contemporary Guatemalan violence.

David McCreery (1988) has written about what happened in 1898 in San Juan with admirable attention to detail. Disputes over land, he observes, were nothing new to the township, which during the colonial period had been involved in such litigation with two of its neighbours, Nebaj and Soloma. Problems were exacerbated, however, with the advent of the Liberal reforms. McCreery notes, like Stoll and Davis, that because of "often shaky bases for claims," titling was not only elaborate and costly but also extremely risky, a legal process "into which the villages, in the absence of any immediate threat, entered reluctantly."

San Juan was forced into legal proceedings by a claim laid in 1893 by Ladino members of the army reserve at Chiantla. Represented by one Mariano García, the Chiantla *milicianos* were listened to favourably. They couched their application in Liberal parlance, stressing "progress" and "private property," key words that fell on government ears with more sympathy than San Juan's petition, lodged on the basis of "ancient titles" and exploitation of land "since time immemorial." As with Santa Eulalia, the claimants from Chiantla counted on government recognition that it was militia like themselves that functioned "as the state's chief instrument of coercion and control in the countryside." At stake in San Juan was land that lay south of the town centre towards Chiantla, part of an allotment of 250 *caballerías* that San Juan claimed exclusively as its own.

San Juan's claim drew a storm of protest not just from Chiantla but also from Soloma and Nebaj. To advance their case the leaders of San Juan sought the services of an engineer, whom they recruited to conduct a survey that was to be paid for by selling community labour. Using the agent Friedrich Koch they arranged a contract for men from San Juan to work on a *finca* called Buenos Aires "in return for the *finca* paying the costs of the land survey," giving Koch as collateral what land titles San Juan already possessed, as well as other relevant documentation. When it appeared that the results of the survey were not to San Juan's advantage, the community refused to take part in any further deliberation. Tempers flared—Ladino *milicianos* from Soloma, it was alleged, laid hands on San Juan's leaders— and discontent grew.

Discontent burst into bloodshed on the evening of July 18, 1898. Failing to acknowledge that the titling process had not been resolved, agents from Finca Buenos Aires arrived in San Juan and began harassing for labour. The people of San Juan believed that the condition upon which their toil had been pledged had yet to be met; thus there was no question of them leaving for the coast. Still the agents pressed. Indians from outlying parts of San Juan arrived in town, adding their resentment to the anger of those already assembled. After the agents had retired to their sleeping quarters in the town hall, the building was set on fire. As they fled the flames the agents were attacked and killed. Thinking, in McCreery's words, "to eliminate hostile witnesses and conceal their crime," the crowd then "spread through the village, killing ladino men, women, and children" in addition to "abusing and threatening" those Indians who had co-operated with the agents. When, by morning, it became clear that some agents or their associates had escaped, San Juan steeled itself for retaliation.

It came swiftly from both north and south. Soloma and Chiantla sent in their militia, which according to McCreery caused "an unknown number" of Indian deaths. Some sixty individuals were sent to stand trial in Huehuetenango. While McCreery finds "no evidence that the government specifically stripped San Juan of its land as punishment," he observes that "in the aftermath of the violence the inhabitants were in a weak position to defend their rights." The *milicianos* of Chiantla eventually received 113 *caballerías* near Tocal. Others from Soloma did equally well. As with Ladino successes in Barillas and the Ixcán, those residents of Chiantla and Soloma who were awarded title "did little to develop their new properties," preferring instead to convince "existing residents to stay," recruit "new ones where possible," and simply live off rents "while waiting for the land to appreciate in value."

They did not have long to wait. Within a few years the successful claimants resold land to plantation owners on the Pacific slope. The new owners required rent to be paid not in cash or in kind but in labour, thus creating a situation in which "workers' estates" in the highlands supplied lowland plantations with a seasonal supply of workers. San Juan never ceased to dispute the legitimacy of the grip plantation owners exerted over community land: "We don't know how it came into the hands of the *fincas*," townspeople lamented in one communication. Over the course of the next thirty years, McCreery writes, San Juan sustained "a steady and largely non-violent, but certainly not passive resistance to the *finca* properties in their midst." Not until the late 1940s were the "workers' estates" dismantled and the native estate delivered back into Maya hands.

---

What, in sum, can be said to have occurred in Guatemala during the century after independence? Despite their physical and psychological seclusion, Maya communities between 1821 and 1920 were exposed to the same historical forces that prevailed in Spanish America as a whole.

The first half-century after independence, especially under the Conservative regime of Rafael Carrera, saw Maya life continue to unfold for the most part within the culture of refuge that had crystallized during colonial times. Whether neglected or protected by the policies of Carrera, Maya communities could not help but be affected by the radical change in how Guatemala was governed after 1871, when Liberals held power. The presidency of Justo Rufino Barrios in particular signalled dramatic and unprecedented change as Guatemala was transformed from a colonial backwater into a modern capitalist nation, primarily on the basis of the commercial production of coffee. To the state, coffee represented progress, civilization, and advancement; to Maya communities it meant loss of land and forced or indentured labour.

The four Cuchumatán case studies indicate that, at the local or community level, the outcome of the Liberal reforms was nuanced and variable. Santiago Chimaltenango appears to have been affected only minimally, Nebaj significantly more. Santa Eulalia and San Juan Ixcoy both suffered considerably—San Juan with the additional consequences of state retribution after a bloody uprising. Differences in the degree of impact and opposition characterize other parts of Guatemala as well. Inequalities that began to emerge at the national level in the nineteenth century have yet to be redressed, especially in the Indian countryside. There, land is life. To deprive Maya communities of land is to deprive them of life.

# CHAPTER NINETEEN

# The T-Shirt Parade

L EONARDO BUCH CHIROY doesn't quite *look* like the Maya Indian he truly is, at least compared to the exotic images that greet passengers who arrive at Aurora airport in Guatemala City. It's his clothes that do it, especially the T-shirt, which hangs loosely over a pair of jeans and gives his outward appearance a distinct, otherworldly dimension. The words on the T-shirt are familiar but a bit disorienting: BEAM ME UP, SCOTTY, they declare. How many Maya Trekkies are there in Guatemala? Beats me, but I spotted and spoke with at least one.

Leonardo is a teenager from San Jorge la Laguna, a Kaqchikel community lying off the road half-way between Sololá and Panajachel. We look down at San Jorge from the *mirador*, or viewpoint, which cars and buses stop at so their passengers can behold the majesty of Lake Atitlán, still beautiful despite the ravages of modern tourism. It's from the tourist trade that Leonardo, like many Mayas, tries to make a living. He sells jewellery—rings, necklaces, bracelets, and earrings—to passing travellers. One of his customers negotiated in kind, hence Leonardo's Star Trek apparel.

I ask Leonardo if he understands what the words on his T-shirt refer to. "Something to do with your gods," he replies. Not quite but pretty close, I say to myself. He sees my camera. "Want me to take your photo?" He clicks the small red button like a pro. "You can take one of me if you like. Only *send* it to me. People take photos of us all the time"—he gestures to his two sisters, both younger than him and both wearing colourful Maya clothes—"but they never send anything back, even though they say they will."

The chance encounter convinces me to keep my eyes peeled, for I've noticed T-shirts, those global articles of clothing, being worn in Guatemala more and more these days, usually by Maya men, not Maya women, which is the case with Leonardo and his sisters. I decide to wait until I get to Chichicastenango, where I am to attend an international conference on sustainable development, before I put my observational skills into systematic operation.

The conference proves to be of variable quality and mixed interest. I enjoy the presentations of several participants very much, a handful of Maya delegates among them. Their inclusion in the program serves to ground discussions of culture and identity, a welcome respite from the abstract, irrelevant, or naive musings of other speakers. By the third evening I'm restless. The following morning I decide to spend my time not listening to papers but exploring town instead.

A huge billboard on the way to Chichicastenango, advertising cigarettes, labels the place the "Mecca of Tourism." Each Thursday and Sunday hordes of tourists, lured by willing native accomplices, engulf Chichicastenango and give market day there a pushy, commercial air. I find Chichicastenango at its enigmatic best the day before market is held, when the locals may be readying the place for imminent invasion but when the town feels more relaxed, the hustle and hype less obvious.

I walk the few blocks from my hotel to the church, choosing not to enter by climbing up the front steps but by skirting around them to a side doorway that leads into the courtyard of the former Dominican convent. Here it was, at the turn of the eighteenth century, that Francisco Ximénez, then parish priest of Chichicastenango, was first shown the *Popol Vuh*, the "Bible of America," a K'iche' Maya account of the creation of the universe. The *Popol Vuh* records a rich multiplicity of knowledge, including myths, legends, memories of historic migrations, and tales of lineage wars, from the days of the first ancestors to the arrival in Guatemala of the first Spaniards. It is a document, and a symbol, of Maya survival. A plaque on a wall commemorates Father Ximénez and the *Popol Vuh*. After I read it I pass from the courtyard into the church through a side entrance.

It takes my eyes a few seconds to adjust to the dim, crepuscular interior. I notice a group of people gathered beneath a statue of the

Virgin to the left of the main altar. Mothers and daughters are dressed in *huipiles*, dextrously woven Maya blouses, and thick wraparound skirts. They have brought armfuls of flowers with them to show their devotion. A man I take to be husband and father lights candles and burns incense while mumbling a prayer in K'iche'. Smoke from his offering hovers over the huddled assembly. I move closer to get a good look at the T-shirt he's wearing. On it the flag of the United States flies above a military convoy. Beneath the stars and stripes are the words OPERATION DESERT STORM: THESE COLORS DON'T RUN. The man's facial features—the high cheek bones, the hooked nose, the flat, broad forehead—could have been lifted from a stelae at Quiriguá. I check my watch: a quarter past eight.

I leave the family to their worship and walk the short distance to the graveyard at the western edge of town. Out of nowhere a drunk appears and starts to pester me. I pay him no attention, for I've noticed two old men having a conversation on the Calle Cementerio just across the street from the Comedor Lastor and the Tienda El Minino. They address each other not in Spanish but in K'iche'. One of them wears a grubby, tattered T-shirt that announces YOU'VE COME A LONG WAY BABY. The other is more smartly turned out, as one would expect, for his T-shirt reads IT'S HARD BEING SEXY, BUT SOMEONE HAS TO DO IT. I glance at my watch: eight fifty-five. Time for breakfast.

I make my way to La Fonda del Tzijolaj, named (so the waiter tells me) after the horse that leads a religious procession during the fiesta of Santo Tomás, the patron saint of Chichicastenango. The restaurant is on the upper level of a building with a commanding view of the central plaza, already showing signs, on Wednesday morning, of preparing for tomorrow's influx. I spot a young man, fifteen or sixteen years of age, starting to erect a market stall. On the front of his T-shirt is the unmistakable figure of Mickey Mouse. He turns around. Guess what? That's right! Who else but Minnie Mouse on the back. Someone steps up to lend a hand with the market stall. The helper seems to prefer American superheroes to Disney cartoon mice, for it's a Batman T-shirt he's wearing.

As I'm eating breakfast a loudspeaker starts blaring. The voice belongs not to an evangelical preacher, of whom there must be hundreds in Chichicastenango alone, but to a used clothes vendor. "*Ropa barata, ropa barata. Dos piezas por un quetzal. Ropa barata, ropa barata.* . . . Cheap clothes, cheap clothes. Two items for twenty cents. Cheap clothes, cheap clothes." I trace the sound of the sales pitch to a white Dodge van parked by El Calvario, the Indian chapel that sits across the central plaza from the church of Santo Tomás. Curiosity takes me there after breakfast.

The vendor, about eighteen years of age, turns out to be an enterprising young Ladino from Guatemala City. He sports a long-sleeved Doobie Brothers T-shirt, from the tour whose message must have been TAKING IT TO THE STREETS. I ask him about his business. He tells me that used clothing enters Guatemala in bulk from the United States, flown into Guatemala City from Miami. His contacts allow him a share of the delivery, which he loads up and "takes to the streets," not only of Chichicastenango but of other towns also. "*Somos muchos.* . . . There's lots of us," he says. And lots of customers too, I comment, observing a number of people picking their way through the vast piles laid on the ground on sheets of plastic. Sure enough, there's plenty of T-shirts in today's batch. The vendor, who sips a 7-Up even though his baseball cap declares a preference for Coca-Cola, reaches for the microphone inside his van. His sales pitch becomes somewhat more refined, broadcast with a subtle hint of solidarity: "*Para nuestra gente de pocos recursos, ropa, dos piezas por un quetzal.* . . . For those of our people with limited resources, clothing, two items for twenty cents." He smiles and waves as I leave. Out of the corner of my eye I spot someone selling ice cream, Helados Donald Duck, who wears a T-shirt saying I'M ONE OF THE PARKWAY SCHOOLKIDS.

I walk back to the church and along Fifth Avenue, also called Gucumatz Avenue, named after a K'iche' forefather. On the steps outside the *auxiliadora*, the Indian municipal office, I talk with a man selling honey. He identifies himself as a *maxeño*, a local term for an inhabitant of Chichicastenango. I point to his T-shirt, a plain affair on which the letters UIMC are printed. "What do these letters stand for?" I inquire. "*Saber*," he replies. "No idea. I just wear the thing." While we talk, four Maya men saunter past in quick succession. All of their T-shirts relate to places far removed from Chichicastenango: CABLE CAR, SAN FRANCISCO; FLAMINGO BAR, FLORIDA; MAUI, HAWAII; and EXPO 86. Wasn't that the one held in Vancouver?

On the way back to my hotel I watch an army patrol move along

Sixth Avenue. A clock strikes ten. I count thirteen soldiers, all of whom look Maya to me. I can't make out what kind of T-shirts they wear underneath their combat fatigues.

I clean up and get ready to head off for the conference, which is being held in plush surroundings in a new hotel on the outskirts of town. First I have to get the pick-up I'm driving, parked in a compound adjacent to my more centrally located hotel. But the pick-up is hemmed in by an enormous truck dropping off a load of firewood. There's a driver at the wheel. "Could you move back a little so I can get out?" I ask him politely. He scowls, jumps down from the cabin, and barks an order to the group of men unloading the firewood. The words are uttered in quickfire K'iche'. He's wearing a marvellous Joe Cocker T-shirt. With a little help from my friends, I manoeuvre the pick-up out to the street.

I drive to the conference wondering what and when my next T-shirt encounter will be. Just before I enter the main auditorium a waiter arrives with a tray of coffee, which he lays down on a nearby table. His name tag informs me that he is called Juan. "That's an interesting T-shirt, Juan," I remark as he pours me a coffee. "Mind if I ask where you got it?"

Juan is forthcoming. "*Es un regalo de mi tío.* . . . A present from my uncle. He gave it to me last year at fiesta time. He lives in California. He left Chichi when I was just a kid. He's been gone twelve years now, but he always comes back home in December for the fiesta of Santo Tomás." Juan's T-shirt depicts a worried-looking dog sitting in an armchair watching television. The dog's head is bandaged and one of its legs is portrayed as an arm, held protectively in a sling. Strewn about the dog are guns and rifles and rounds of ammunition. The words on the T-shirt say LIVING IN L.A.: BE READY. Juan's uncle, it seems, is one of the countless Mayas who prefer a life in exile to a life in Guatemala. I hope he lives there under less duress than the embattled dog.

I'm blethering away with Juan, who tells me he's a *maxeño*, when Demetrio Cojtí Cuxil comes out of the auditorium and asks for a coffee. We exchange greetings. Demetrio's mother is from Chichicastenango, but he was born in a Kaqchikel village near Tecpán. He was schooled by Jesuits and has the distinction of being the first self-identified Maya from Guatemala to earn a doctorate. An alert, quirky individual, Demetrio was one of the first Mayas to teach at the Universidad de San Carlos, Guatemala's national university. He currently works for UNICEF. Anthropologist Carol Smith considers him a "prominent spokesperson for today's Maya nationalists." The talk I heard Demetrio give earlier in the week was direct and hard-hitting. In it he stated that Mayas in Guatemala are subjected to an internal colonialism that denigrates and marginalizes native culture. He spoke, nonetheless, of the vitality of Maya culture, of a Maya identity that (in his words) is not only "generic" but also locally articulated, given to nuance and improvisation, above all else "elastic, fluid, flexible."

I mention my T-shirt sightings to Demetrio. He marshals the evidence to make a point. "The only purpose these T-shirts have is to cover the body. Mayas don't identify with them in any meaningful way." I bring up the gender divide. "That's just how it is," he says. "A family usually puts aside more for what women wear than for what men wear. That's an important decision. Even poor people invest in weaving or in buying woven clothing, especially *huipiles*."

Those dazzling Maya blouses, some specialists maintain, are texts as well as textiles, saying something about community origin or affiliation that no T-shirt can possibly capture. Demetrio also makes the point that when repression was fiercest, some men discarded Maya-style clothing in favour of Western attire, for "Indians" and "guerrillas" were often considered synonymous; the abandonment of traditional community dress was a self-protective, not an assimilationist, measure. I notice that Demetrio himself, like several Mayas at the conference, wears a shirt and a jacket tailored along Western lines but made from locally produced cloth.

I make it, eventually, to the last of the morning's presentations. None of them, however, matches the liveliness of the T-shirt parade. After the talks end I return to my hotel to put my thoughts and notes in some kind of order. I'm scribbling away when I recall a passage in Eduardo Galeano's *Book of Embraces*, which I have along with me. I look it up. "Identity is no museum piece sitting stock-still in a display case," Galeano writes, "but rather the endlessly astonishing synthesis of the contradictions of everyday life." I think back to Leonardo Buch Chiroy and the dozen or so T-shirted Mayas I saw in the course of the morning. A general proposition has survived an empirical test.

# CHAPTER TWENTY

# Indians in
# the Backcountry

THE BACKCOUNTRY north of Kingston, Ontario is home to a mix of people who seem to have little in common save for where they happen to live. I know, or know of, lots of backcountry residents: secretaries and factory workers, sheep farmers and beekeepers, carpenters and stonemasons, prison guards and school teachers, potters and painters, weavers and writers, antique dealers and second-hand book buffs, radio producers and freelance editors, draft dodgers and retired generals, hippies from the sixties who went back to the land, and their New-Age nineties equivalent. I figured there also had to be Indians in the backcountry, but I had never met and spoken with any until the day I travelled up to Arden with Apolinario Chile Pixtún and Matías Quex Serech.

Apolinario and Matías arrived at my house in a state of shock. They'd flown into Toronto from Guatemala the day before, and the climatic jolt between south and north in late November was taking its toll. Apolinario in particular looked quite bewildered. "*Qué frío. . . . * I can't believe how cold it is," he said. "And how everything looks so brown and dried out. When I was here just a few months ago the place was warm and green, lush almost." Matías, who had no past experience of Canada with which to gauge the present, simply asked: "*Va a nevar. . . . * Do you think it might snow? I'd like to see snow, I'd like to see snow falling."

They sat down and ate breakfast without taking off their coats. Matías removed his hat. Apolinario kept his on. "That's better," he

sighed midway through his second cup of coffee. The moment
seemed opportune. I said "Why don't you tell me a bit about your-
selves, what you do, why you're here, so I'll have a better idea of
what it is you'll be saying later on." Matías let Apolinario speak first.

Members of the Federation of Councils of Kaqchikel Elders, the
two were engaged in what might best be described as a cultural mis-
sion. Caught up in the tricky business of staking out an agenda that
addresses Maya concerns in Guatemala, their objectives in visiting
Canada were twofold: first, to make contact and establish links with
native groups and associations; and, second, to seek practical rela-
tionships with non-governmental organizations involved in community development, especially projects relating to appropriate
technology, traditional medicine, and midwifery.

Their preoccupations lay with the valorization and revitalization
of Maya culture, and they took pains to distinguish themselves, if
not distance themselves, from the "popular movement." Politics for
them was primarily a question of creating ways in which Maya customs and practices were not simply safeguarded but allowed freedom of expression, indeed encouraged to grow.

Spiritual as well as material considerations had to be attended to,
Apolinario argued, if peace in Guatemala was to have any future.
His business card, inscribed with a Maya glyph depicting a god of
healing, declared him "a naturopath at the service of humanity." He
lives in the countryside near Chimaltenango but holds consulting
hours twice a week in an office on the outskirts of Guatemala City.
His previous visit to Canada was as a guest of the Royal Ontario
Museum in Toronto, where he took part in the opening ceremony
of an exhibit called "Human Body, Human Spirit."

Apolinario's calling prompted me, after breakfast, to ask him if he
and Matías would be prepared to conduct a ceremony of blessing on
my house. "We'll need a glass of water and some perfume," Apolinario said. I dutifully provided the former, Matías the latter, an
enormous bottle of Brut aftershave. Apolinario looked around my
study and unfurled a cloth on top of my desk. On it were embroidered motifs representing the twenty days, and twenty gods, of the
*tzolkin* calendar, a ritual affair that has governed and measured time
for the Maya for over five millennia.

"Where's south?" he asked. I pointed out the front window as he
exchanged his hat for a *tzute*, an all-purpose cloth men tie around

their heads in the style of a buccaneer's bandanna. We kneeled facing south as Apolinario invoked a blessing. After he finished we turned to face north, and Matías took over the invocation. After his turn it was back to Apolinario, facing west. Matías concluded the spoken part of the ceremony, conducted in Kaqchikel, as we knelt facing east.

Both men then stood up and splashed water and aftershave around the room and on top of the embroidered cloth. I presented each of them with a copy of a book I'd written on Guatemala that had been published in Spanish, our lingua franca. They reciprocated with a calendar in which the year A.D. 1995 had been marked out in Maya days as well as in Gregorian ones, the year by their Choltun or Long Count reckoning being 5111, not 1995. I glanced at the dedication Apolinario had written. *"Con cariño al escritor George Lowel,"* I read, dated *"9 Imox Año 5110."*

Running parallel to the twenty days that constitute a Maya month, or *winal*, is a system of numbers, one to thirteen, each of which bestows on any given day a good or bad omen. *Imox* in Kaqchikel means "World" or "Earth Being," usually depicted as a crocodile. Nine is a propitious number, for nine gods are thought to rule the underworld, and nine falls before ten, which Mayas dread, for it is associated with Death. I took *9 Imox* to be a good day, one worthy of celebration. I fetched a prized bottle of single-malt whisky. "People in my country call this the water of life," I said. "Would you care for a glass before we set off?" Apolinario exclaimed, *"Ay, qué bueno!"* and dispatched his dram with alacrity.

The hour or so we spent on the road saw us travel through a landscape gnawed to the bone by nature and season. Trees were gaunt and bare, the fields around them stripped of growth. Lakes were still, the sky above them emitting a washed-out pearly light. I wondered what it must be like to behold such topography through Maya eyes, for even in the dry season the highlands of Guatemala would seem, by comparison, verdant and inviting.

Our hosts, all members of Ardoch Algonquin First Nation and Allies, greeted us warmly. The band consists of some 220 registered members, and eight of them were present at Marlene Tsun's house, a tin-sided structure on the lonely main street of Arden. "You made it," Marlene said with relief. "We were starting to get worried." She introduced us to her husband Wade, an artist, and led us into the living room where others were waiting: Kathleen and Fred Antoine, the

latter a community elder; Bob Lovelace, a Cherokee now living near
Sharbot Lake; Harold Perry, community spokesperson; and Dorothy
and Frank Antoine, the latter the son of Fred, from whom he takes his
leadership qualities. I introduced the Mayas, then started translating
back and forth from English into Spanish, from Spanish into English.
It was more an intermingling than a confusion of tongues, but there
were moments during the hours that followed when communication
across cultures was better served by other means than words.

Dialogue, however, was revealing, at times determining broad
bases of similarity, at times throwing differences into sharp relief.
"How you feel about corn is the way we feel about wild rice,"
Dorothy observed. "It's a sacred food for us. The wild rice we gather
we share and eat. We don't sell it." Harold looked almost taken
aback when Apolinario mentioned how many Maya languages were
spoken by how many Maya people. "Over twenty languages? Languages, not dialects?" he asked. Since none of our guests had been
raised speaking Algonquin, though some are now learning it, it
seemed remarkable to think of five million people speaking Maya.

A delicious meal had been prepared—wild rice and chicken—
but before it was served Frank performed a smudging ceremony. A
bowl on the coffee table was lit, its contents of tobacco, sage, cedar,
and sweetgrass crackling to life and sending off pleasant, aromatic
wafts. Frank moved his hands through the grey vapour, up to and
over his face, in a slow, circular rhythm. "We smudge to connect
with the Creator," he said, "and to be in touch with the ancestors. It
also cleanses us spiritually." We all smudged in turn, then ate.

After the meal the dialogue continued, topics ranging from land
rights to native education, from canoeing and fishing to the colours
associated with the cardinal directions. Before we left Apolinario
said that he too, like Frank, would like to perform a smudging ceremony, one that would symbolize solidarity and express appreciation.
He produced a larger bowl than Frank's, filling it with *pom*, a
resinous incense, and a blend of medicinal plants and herbs. The
pyrotechnics were spectacular. Clouds billowed up across the living
room, sparks flew over the coffee table on to the floor, Marlene's cat
scampered, and the smoke detector began to wail. Once Wade had
silenced the alarm Apolinario chanted a prayer.

On the road back to Kingston, Matías's wish was granted: it
snowed, thick soft flakes from a glittering sky.

# *Epilogue*

THE CAPTION on the calendar at a friend's house catches my eye: "1995—The Year of Peace." It is only my first week back in Guatemala, but nothing I have heard or read warrants such an assertion. In Guatemala, declaring peace does not mean the end of war.

A special "Peace Supplement" in the April 30 issue of *Prensa Libre* shares the calendar's optimism. "When the guns fall silent and peace breaks out," *Prensa Libre* says, "Guatemalans will say goodbye to thirty-four years of armed conflict. The task, then, will be to look to the future, determined to avoid a new struggle between brother and brother."

How, I ask myself, can a "new struggle" be avoided if the root causes of civil war are talked about, year after year, administration after administration, only to be addressed in theory, not in practice? The "firm and lasting peace agreement" scheduled to be signed in December 1994 never materialized. Instead, the government and guerrilla representatives agreed on another round of peace talks. Talking about peace may be the closest Guatemala ever gets to it.

President Ramiro De León Carpio epitomizes the gulf between rhetoric and reality. In an interview published in the news magazine *Crónica* in May the president expresses his belief that, when 1995 ends, he will have passed on to his successor "an entirely different scenario" than the one he inherited when he took office. A public relations campaign mounted in the Guatemalan press is meant to portray De León's government in a positive light. Four well-intentioned announcements in several newspapers serve equally well as a form of self-indictment. They run:

> **CONDEMNED TO IGNORANCE:** Lack of education in our country impedes our social and economic development. Fifty-four per cent of our population are illiterate.

> **CONDEMNED TO FEAR:** Each day our country experiences a high number of assassinations, the result of common delinquency. For every one thousand inhabitants we have only one police officer.

> **CONDEMNED TO ISOLATION:** The absence of roads and bridges marginalizes many of our communities, restricting their commercial and economic development. We lose as much as 20 per cent of what small farmers produce each year because of inadequate infrastructure.

> **CONDEMNED TO DEATH:** A shortage of health services causes us to have one of the highest rates of infant mortality in Latin America. Only one in three Guatemalans has access to medical facilities.

All four announcements appear alongside related images—a tired teenager at work in the fields; a street urchin huddled anxiously on a bench; a young girl carrying corn in a basket on her head; a crying, malnourished child—and they all impart the same simplistic, remedial message: "In order for the Value Added Tax you pay to be channelled into works that benefit everyone, ask for a receipt or a record of payment, because whoever defrauds Guatemala defrauds and condemns you."

As worthy as this initiative may be, far more deserving of government attention is non-payment of property taxes or failure to ensure that workers receive a legally established minimum daily wage. Insisting that an intransigent elite assume some measure of fiscal and financial responsibility does not constitute an excessive demand, given the taboo status of land reform, but De León Carpio dodges these issues as resolutely as any of his predecessors.

If Guatemala's economic elite continues to evade the moral obligation to pay their taxes and disburse fair wages, a flicker of hope now exists that members of another powerful group—the military—may at last be brought to account for past crimes. Revelations in March 1995 that Colonel Julio Roberto Alpírez, a senior officer in the Guatemalan armed forces, was involved in the June 1990 murder of a U.S. citizen, Michael DeVine, shocked senators and members of Congress in Washington but caused little commotion in Guatemala. American indignation grew when it was further revealed that Alpírez, a graduate of the U.S. Army's School of the Americas in Fort Benning, Georgia, was on the payroll of the Central Intelligence Agency at the time of DeVine's murder, which took place near Poptún, where DeVine owned an inn. The CIA relieved Alpírez of his duties in July 1992—the colonel received a severance payment of $44,000—only after he was implicated in a second murder, that of the Guatemalan guerrilla leader Efraín Bámaca. Bámaca is alleged to have died under torture, if not at Alpírez's hands then under the colonel's direct supervision as commanding officer of the army base in San Marcos. Bámaca was detained there following his capture in March 1992.

Bámaca was married to Jennifer Harbury, a U.S. lawyer whose pursuit of justice has brought to light multiple irregularities. One is that the CIA continued to finance army intelligence units in Guatemala even though President George Bush ordered a halt to all military assistance to Guatemala because of a lack of co-operation in investigation of the DeVine case. On March 23, 1995, Harbury issued a statement that cuts to the heart of the matter:

> I am saddened but not at all surprised to hear of the direct link with the CIA in the assassination of my husband. I have lived in Guatemala for two years, and have been closely involved with that country for a decade now. Over and over again, I have seen the direct linkage with an obvious support for the Guatemalan army, which has long been labelled the worst human rights violator in the western hemisphere. Our Department of State has long sheltered, supported, and trained this army, and helped to cover up for its terrible and criminal acts. As a result, its impunity has grown stronger and stronger, and 150,000 civilians lie dead. We, the citizens of the United States, must now insist that our tax dollars be better spent.

Harbury gives her personal loss an all-important collective dimension:

> I ask that all of us, here in the United States, recognize that I am
> but one of hundreds of thousands of women across Latin Amer-
> ica who have suffered the grim experience of searching for a
> loved one who has been "disappeared" by the authorities. Many
> such women in Guatemala are in fact my close friends. Unlike
> them, I have been given the privilege of at last knowing the
> truth, and being freed from the constant nightmare that my hus-
> band is being tortured. Others have received no such relief. . . . I
> must now learn where my husband is buried, and return to
> Guatemala to reclaim his body. I cannot leave him tossed like so
> much trash into an unmarked grave. His bones belong to me.

Alpírez, who denies both charges of murder and any remunera-
tive association with the CIA, was suspended from duty on April 27,
1995, along with fellow colonel Mario García Catalán, also implicated in the DeVine affair. Robert Torricelli, the U.S. congressman
responsible for exposing Alpírez's connections, has called for the
colonel's extradition and prosecution in a U.S. court of law. President De León Carpio's advice to Alpírez prior to his suspension was
to sue Torricelli for defamation of character.

Whether or not Alpírez is eventually put on trial, it is clear that
the courage found to lodge a case against him will also be drawn
upon to press charges against other members of the Guatemalan military. The Grupo de Apoyo Mutuo, a human rights association,
intends to bring a suit against Alpírez because of his involvement in a
series of abductions in 1984. Another human rights group, the Aso-
ciación de Familiares de Detenidos-Desaparecidos (FAMDEGUA),
plans to charge army officers with responsibility for the massacre
committed in 1982 in the Petén district of La Libertad, where thirteen sets of bones were exhumed from a village well in July 1994.
Aura Elena Farfán, a FAMDEGUA spokesperson, says that "the soldiers
were most astute, for after they killed some villagers, they stripped
them of their clothes, and put them on." The soldiers apparently did
this in a deliberate attempt to conceal their identity as they set about
killing other village residents.

"But the soldiers forgot to change their boots," Farfán observes, and this gave them away. The soldiers in question were stationed at the army base in Las Cruces under the command of Captain Carlos Carías. Farfán, quoted in the *Prensa Libre* of May 6, 1995, adds: "We intend to keep going until we find our loved ones, even if all we find are their remains. We seek justice, not revenge. Without justice it is impossible to speak of peace and reconciliation."

Farfán's stance is supported by Archbishop Próspero Penados del Barrio, who has committed the Catholic Church to a social project called the Recovery of Historical Memory, designed to put on record details of atrocities carried out in Guatemala in the 1980s. The Church's project will benefit enormously from the work of the Equipo de Antropología Forense de Guatemala (EAFG), a forensic science team that in 1994 exhumed eighty-four bodies from a clandestine cemetery in what was once Plan de Sánchez, a small rural community near the town of Rabinal. If the evidence from Plan de Sánchez is anything to judge by—*Prensa Libre* carried a full-page account on April 30, 1995—eyewitness testimony is available to corroborate clinical findings. Stefan Schmitt, a member of EAFG and the person in charge of the exhumation, had this to say:

> Our investigation reveals that death was brought about by a violent attack which involved the use of grenades, firearms, and hand weapons such as blades and bayonets. Most bodies were also badly burned. In the course of excavation we found splinters from grenades as well as the cartridge shells of 5.56 calibre bullets, the kind used in Galil and M-16 rifles. In addition, some bones exhibited marks characteristically made by the thrust of a knife. Others showed signs of sustained beating. Of the eighty-four sets of remains, five belonged to persons three years of age or less, seventeen belonged to persons between four and twelve years of age, seventeen belonged to persons between thirteen and twenty-two years of age, forty belonged to persons between twenty-three and forty-nine years of age, and five belonged to persons fifty years of age or more.

After exhumation, twenty-five people were identified by name and their age at death established. They ranged from seven to eighty-eight years of age. Many of them were members of the same family or closely related. These people, and perhaps over 150 of their neighbours, were massacred on Sunday, July 18, 1982, as market day in Plan de Sánchez drew to a close. Salvador García Sánchez, aged fifteen at the time, was there:

> The women were all dressed up in their best clothes and people from all around had brought in their corn to sell at market. An army patrol, twenty-five soldiers in all, left the barracks in Rabinal about three o'clock in the afternoon and headed towards Plan de Sánchez. They laid siege to the community, surrounding it so that no one could leave. They locked people up—old people, men, women, and children—in the house of my cousin, Rosa Manuel Jerónimo, right in the heart of the community. They took twelve young girls to a place where no one lived, raped them, tortured them, and then killed them.

The house in which people were locked up, according to Adrián Cajbón Jerónimo, who also saw what happened, was then struck by grenades, strafed by gunfire, and set alight. "When the house was engulfed by flames, the soldiers threw in more people," Cajbón says. "That night 180 people died. The fire didn't go out until six o'clock the following morning."

On April 29, 1995, almost thirteen years after they died, eighty-four victims of the massacre at Plan de Sánchez were laid side by side in rustic wooden coffins before the main altar of the Church of San Mateo Apóstol in Salamá. The Bishop of Baja Verapaz, Oscar García Urízar, presided over a special mass in which Catholic and Maya rites were both observed. Monseñor García looked down on the eighty-four coffins in front of him.

"I am ashamed and feel the sorrow that the relatives of the dead must feel," he said. "It is degrading to behold the savagery resorted to by men who would govern us."

The man who governed Guatemala when the people of Plan de Sánchez were slaughtered was General Efraín Ríos Montt. According to a survey published in *La República* the day before Monseñor García said mass, Ríos Montt was the first-choice candidate of 38 per cent of all those polled, ten percentage points ahead of his closest rival, for the 1995 presidential election.

# Sources and Commentary

P EOPLE began to write about what is now Guatemala a long
time ago. Our oldest records, those left by the Maya themselves, are in the form of hieroglyphic inscriptions that,
according to Gordon Brotherston (1992), appear on various artifacts
dating from as early as A.D. 300. For six centuries thereafter, Classic
Maya culture expressed itself textually on the surface of alabaster,
bone, jade, obsidian, onyx, paper, pottery, shell, stone, and wood.
Scripts from the Classic period (A.D. 300 to 900) are rich and plentiful compared with the meagre survivals of the Postclassic (A.D. 900-
1524).

Since the time of Sylvanus G. Morley (1915) and J. Eric S.
Thompson (1960), the interpretation of Maya writing has been rev-
olutionized by the work of Michael D. Coe (1992), Ian Graham
(1975), Stephen D. Houston (1989), David H. Kelley (1976), Linda
Schele and David Freidel (1990), and Linda Schele and Mary E.
Miller (1986). To Tatiana Proskouriakoff (1960) goes much of the
credit for shifting the research focus of Maya archaeology away from
issues of astronomy, cosmology, and the contemplation of time (see
León-Portilla 1988) to the more mundane operation of war and politics, especially the rise and fall of dynastic rulers and city states.

Conquest by imperial Spain saw Maya peoples in Guatemala
adapt their ways of writing to European conventions, which meant
learning how to use the Latin alphabet. The practice, begun in the
mid-sixteenth century, resulted in the preservation of all sorts of

knowledge that allows us to see how the world looks through Maya eyes. Numerous texts exist, the most famous being the *Popol Vuh*, translated directly from K'iche' into English by Munro S. Edmonson (1971) and Dennis Tedlock (1985). Delia Goetz and Sylvanus G. Morley also provide access to the *Popol Vuh* in English, via the Spanish translation of Adrián Recinos (1950). Another key text is the *Annals of the Cakchiquels*, which Daniel G. Brinton (1885) and Recinos and Goetz (1953) translated directly from Kaqchikel into English. Robert M. Carmack (1973) provides the best available guide to these and other indigenous documents.

In English-language historiography, Mayas and Spaniards first appear in print courtesy of Thomas Gage, whose experiences in Guatemala in the seventeenth century make fascinating reading. Gage's portrayal of the Maya lot, like the cleric himself, is not without its blemishes and idiosyncrasies, but his first-hand observations of conquest in action are striking, if not entirely trustworthy. A.P. Newton (1928) tampers with Gage's righteous, self-serving text far less than does J. Eric S. Thompson (1958). Two centuries passed before another Englishman, Henry Dunn, published an account of his year-long stay in Guatemala. Dunn (1829) has worthwhile insights, but it was the American traveller John Lloyd Stephens (1841) who opened up the Maya world as never before. Stephens forged a literary genre that influenced the likes of Anne and Alfred Maudslay (1899), Thomas Gann (1926), and Aldous Huxley (1934) and that is venerated in our day by Ronald Wright (1989), Anthony Daniels (1990), and Peter Canby (1992), among others less engaging.

Scholarly studies that situate Guatemala in the Spanish scheme of empire tend to be overshadowed by the literature available on Mexico; the lands and peoples conquered by Cortés, it seems, were destined to attract greater attention than those conquered by Pedro de Alvarado (Mackie 1924). Murdo J. MacLeod (1973) has served as the landmark work on colonial Guatemala for two decades and will most likely serve a similar purpose for years to come. William L. Sherman (1979) fills a large gap in our awareness of how Spaniards controlled and exploited the indigenous population. Miles L. Wortman (1982) emphasizes economic and social matters, while Adriaan C. van Oss (1986) concentrates on the role of the Church. Christopher H. Lutz (1994) furnishes us with a vivid urban history of Santiago de Guatemala, and the art and architecture of that city receive detailed treatment at the hands of Sidney D. Markman (1966) and Verle L. Annis (1968). Ralph H. Vigil (1987) charts the life and times of Alonso de Zorita, a Crown official who toiled to impose government authority in the mid-sixteenth century by enforcing laws aimed at improving Indian welfare. Wendy Kramer (1994) sheds new light on those turbulent first years of conquest. Robert M. Carmack (1981), Nancy M. Farriss (1984), Robert M. Hill (1991), Grant D. Jones (1989), and Sandra L. Orellana (1984) examine at length the fate of Maya peoples under Spanish rule. My own research endeavours, alone or in collaboration with others (Cook and Lovell 1992; Lovell 1992; Lovell and Lutz 1995; Lovell and Swezey 1990), assess the cultural and demographic repercussions of conquest. Readers who want to track down the provenance of sources quoted in chapters 1 and 17 here are referred to these works for archival or bibliographic particulars. Michael Taussig (1984, 1987) addresses with dazzling virtuosity the fears and terror tactics that charge all colonial encounters, as do Inga Clendinnen (1987), Paul Sullivan (1989), and Dennis Tedlock (1993).

For the nineteenth and early twentieth centuries, E. Bradford Burns (1980, 1985), David McCreery (1990, 1994), and Ralph Lee Woodward, Jr. (1990, 1993) help empiricize the more conceptual schema of Oliver La Farge (1940), Robert A. Naylor (1967), and Carol A. Smith (1984). Robert G. Williams (1994) sets the emergence of Guatemala as a "coffee republic" in a comparative Central American context. The case studies presented in chapter 18 are derived from the work of several scholars: Charles Wagley (1941, 1949) and John M. Watanabe (1990, 1992) on Santiago Chimaltenango; Robert Burkitt (1930), Jackson S. Lincoln (1945), Benjamin Colby and Pierre van den Berghe (1969), and David Stoll (1993) on Nebaj; Oliver La Farge (1947) and Shelton H. Davis (1970) on Santa Eulalia; and David McCreery (1988) on San Juan Ixcoy.

The so-called Guatemalan Revolution of 1944-54—and especially what a decade of rural conflict and agrarian reform represented for Maya communities—is open to at least two interpretations. In terms of popular gains, Robert Wasserstrom (1975) believes it amounted to very little; Jim Handy (1994) champions the opposite view. Handy's study is more cogently argued and more thoroughly researched than Wasserstrom's. Handy stresses an array of internal factors as much if not more than the part played by external agents.

Interference in Guatemalan affairs by the U.S. government and corporate interests is well documented by Richard Immerman (1982)
and Piero Gleijeses (1991). The words of Ambassador John Peuri-
foy's wife and of President Arbenz, quoted in chapter 4, can be
found in the damning exposé of Stephen Schlesinger and Stephen
Kinzer (1982).

Coming to grips with the four decades of political turmoil that
have scarred Guatemala since the overthrow of Arbenz is no easy
task. Richard N. Adams (1970) is a useful point of departure and
contains trenchant remarks about power structures and the modern
military establishment. Eduardo Galeano (1969) remains an indis-
pensable source for examining key events of the 1960s, with Tom
Barry (1995), George Black (1984), Duncan Green (1992), Jim
Handy (1984), Susanne Jonas (1991), Deborah Levenson-Estrada
(1994), James Painter (1987), Victor Perera (1993), Jennifer
Schirmer (1995), Jean-Marie Simon (1987), and Robert H. Trudeau
(1993) steering the reader through more recent upheavals. Robert
M. Carmack (1988) pays special attention to the impact of violence
on Maya peoples, while James Dunkerley (1988, 1994) fits contemporary Guatemalan politics into a larger isthmian scenario. Mario
Payeras (1983) articulates the goals of the guerrilla insurgency; the
Guatemalan Church in Exile (1989) makes public those of the
Guatemalan military, spelled out in chapter 12. From a report published by Cultural Survival and the Anthropology Resource Center
(1983) I lift the gruesome testimony of the massacre that took place
at Finca San Francisco, one of a litany of atrocities chronicled by the
pertinacious Ricardo Falla (1983, 1984, 1994). I have attempted to
indicate, chapter by chapter, the newspaper sources that inform
much of part 2. On the second floor of the National Library in
Guatemala City, the Hemeroteca Nacional strives to maintain its
impressive collection of newspapers and periodicals, which dates
back to the nineteenth century. Anyone who seeks out these sources
needs to be wary and alert. Newspapers in Guatemala, observes a
character in Francisco Goldman's novel *The Long Night of White
Chickens* (1992), "have to be read to be believed." There are times I
would prefer *not* to believe what I read in the Guatemalan press, but
that would constitute an act of denial I choose to avoid.

Anthropological research on Guatemala has produced many distinguished contributions, often set in the context of one specific

Maya community. The best community studies show an awareness of the importance of history, even if many float ungrounded in a timeless ethnographic present. Four collections of essays—those edited by Clarence L. Hay et al. (1940), Sol Tax (1950), Carl Kendall, John Hawkins, and Laurel Bossen (1983), and Victoria R. Bricker and Gary H. Gossen (1989)—allow an appraisal to be made of how the state of the art has evolved. The talented Maud Oakes (1951a,b) crafted not one but two classic accounts. Oliver La Farge can be credited with three: one as sole author (1947); one working with Frans Blom (1926, 1927); and another with Douglas Byers (1931). There are occasions, or so it seems to me, when the postmodern soul-searching of anthropologists (see Watanabe 1995) could profit from a sanguine reading of neglected or forgotten predecessors.

That said, several recent efforts indicate that textual innovation is alive and well, especially when it comes to finding suitable ways for Mayas themselves to participate in the telling of their stories. Working closely with Andrés Xiloj, for example, enabled Dennis Tedlock (1985) to imbue his translation of the *Popol Vuh* with living K'iche' authority. A similar disposition on the part of Barbara Tedlock (1992) permeates her portrayal of how age-old concepts of time and space are kept alive in the daily routines of the present. James D. Sexton (1981, 1985, 1992a,b) facilitates the narration of life history as adroitly as he renders Maya fables and folk tales. Gaspar González (1995), Rigoberta Menchú (1984), and Victor Montejo (1984, 1987, 1991) speak to us more directly, three Maya voices now heard among a growing concert of others (Anderson and Garlock 1988; Hooks 1993; Smith-Ayala 1991). Linda Green (1994) weaves the painful experiences of the women she worked with into an illuminating discussion of fear as a way of life. Richard Wilson (1991, 1993, 1995) does the same for the Q'eqchi' subjects of his fieldwork, whom he sees turning political repression into cultural resurgence. Language and dress (Deuss 1990; Mayers 1966; Schevill 1993; Warren 1994) are rich repositories of culture and identity.

If rebirth and renewal indeed signal a new Maya order (Smith 1991; Warren 1992), the gains have not been achieved without tremendous costs (Smith 1990; Wright 1992). As Mayas regroup and rebuild, they do so remembering not only the dead and the disappeared but also the exiled and the displaced (Manz 1988; Vlach

1992; Burns 1993). Perhaps the writers of the *Popol Vuh* had some form of solace in mind when they recorded: "Whatever might be is simply not there: only murmurs, ripples, in the dark, in the night."

———————————

Adams, Richard N. 1970. *Crucifixion by Power: Essays on Guatemalan National Social Structure, 1944-1966*. Austin: University of Texas Press.

Anderson, Marilyn and Jonathan Garlock, eds. 1988. *Granddaughters of Corn: Portraits of Guatemalan Women*. Willimantic, Conn.: Curbstone Press.

Annis, Verle L. 1968. *The Architecture of Antigua Guatemala*. Guatemala: University of San Carlos Press.

Barry, Tom with Kent Norsworthy. 1995. *Inside Guatemala*. London: Latin America Bureau.

Black, George with Milton Jamail and Norma Stoltz Chinchilla. 1984. *Garrison Guatemala*. New York: Monthly Review Press.

Blom, Frans and Oliver La Farge. 1926, 1927. *Tribes and Temples*. 2 vols. New Orleans: Tulane University Press.

Bricker, Victoria R. and Gary H. Gossen, eds. 1989. *Ethnographic Encounters in Southern Mesoamerica: Essays in Honor of Evon Zartman Vogt, Jr.* Albany, N.Y.: Institute of Mesoamerican Studies.

Brinton, Daniel G. 1885. *The Annals of the Cakchiquels*. Philadelphia: Library of Aboriginal American Literature.

Brotherston, Gordon. 1992. *Book of the Fourth World: Reading the Native Americas through Their Literature*. Cambridge: Cambridge University Press.

Burkitt, Robert. 1930. "Explorations in the Highlands of Western Guatemala," *The Museum Journal*, 21(1): 41-72.

Burns, Allan F. 1993. *Maya in Exile: Guatemalans in Florida*. Philadelphia: Temple University Press.

Burns, E. Bradford. 1980. *The Poverty of Progress: Latin America in the Nineteenth Century*. Berkeley, Los Angeles, and London: University of California Press.

Burns, E. Bradford. 1985. *Eadweard Muybridge in Guatemala, 1975: The Photographer as Social Recorder*. Berkeley, Los Angeles, and London: University of California Press.

Canby, Peter. 1992. *The Heart of the Sky: Travels among the Maya.* New York: HarperCollins Publishers.

Carmack, Robert M. 1973. *Quichean Civilization: The Ethnohistoric, Ethnographic, and Archaeological Sources.* Berkeley, Los Angeles, and London: University of California Press.

Carmack, Robert M. 1981. *The Quiché Mayas of Utatlán: The Evolution of a Highland Guatemalan Kingdom.* Norman: University of Oklahoma Press.

Carmack, Robert M., ed. 1988. *Harvest of Violence: The Maya Indians and the Guatemalan Crisis.* Norman and London: University of Oklahoma Press.

Clendinnen, Inga. 1987. *Ambivalent Conquests: Maya and Spaniard in Yucatán, 1517-1570.* Cambridge: Cambridge University Press.

Coe, Michael D. 1992. *Breaking the Maya Code.* New York: Thames and Hudson.

Colby, Benjamin and Pierre van den Berghe. 1969. *Ixil Country: A Plural Society in Highland Guatemala.* Berkeley, Los Angeles, and London: University of California Press.

Cook, Noble David and W. George Lovell, eds. 1992. *"Secret Judgments of God": Old World Disease in Colonial Spanish America.* Norman and London: University of Oklahoma Press.

Cultural Survival and the Anthropology Resource Center. 1983. *Voices of the Survivors: The Massacre at Finca San Francisco, Guatemala.* Peterborough, N.H.: Transcript Printing Company.

Daniels, Anthony. 1990. *Sweet Waist of America: Journeys around Guatemala.* London: Hutchinson Books.

Davis, Shelton H. 1970. "Land of Our Ancestors: A Study of Land Tenure and Inheritance in the Highlands of Guatemala." Ph.D. dissertation, Harvard University.

Deuss, Krystyna. 1990. *Indian Costumes from Guatemala.* 2nd ed. Nottingham, England: Charles Goater and Son.

Dunkerley, James. 1988. *Power in the Isthmus: A Political History of Modern Central America.* London: Verso.

Dunkerley, James. 1994. *The Pacification of Central America.* London: Verso.

Dunn, Henry. [1829] 1981. *Guatemala, or The Republic of Central America in 1827-8.* Detroit: Blaine Ethridge.

Edmonson, Munro S., trans. 1971. *The Book of Counsel: The Popol Vuh of the Quiché Maya of Guatemala.* New Orleans: Tulane University Press.

Falla, Ricardo. 1983. "The Massacre at the Rural Estate of San Francisco, July 1982," *Cultural Survival Quarterly,* 7(1): 43-44.

Falla, Ricardo. 1984. "We Charge Genocide," in *Guatemala: Tyranny on Trial,* ed. Susanne Jonas, E. McCaughan, and E. Sutherland Martínez. San Francisco: Synthesis.

Falla, Ricardo. 1994. *Massacres in the Jungle: Ixcán, Guatemala, 1975-1982.* Trans. Julia Howland. Boulder, Col., San Francisco, and Oxford: Westview Press.

Farriss, Nancy M. 1984. *Maya Society under Spanish Rule: The Collective Enterprise of Survival.* Princeton, N.J.: Princeton University Press.

Fuentes, Carlos. 1984. *Latin America: At War with the Past.* Toronto: CBC Publications.

Galeano, Eduardo. 1969. *Guatemala: Occupied Country.* Trans. Cedric Belfrage. New York: Monthly Review Press.

Galeano, Eduardo. 1991. *The Book of Embraces.* Trans. Cedric Belfrage, with Mark Schafer. New York and London: W.W. Norton and Company.

Gann, Thomas. 1926. *Ancient Cities and Modern Tribes: Exploration and Adventure in Maya Lands.* London: Duckworth.

Glassman, Paul. 1988. *Guatemala Guide.* Champlain, N.Y.: Passport Press.

Gleijeses, Piero. 1991. *Shattered Hope: The Guatemalan Revolution and the United States, 1944-54.* Princeton, N.J.: Princeton University Press.

Goldman, Francisco. 1992. *The Long Night of White Chickens.* New York: Atlantic Monthly Press.

González, Pedro Gaspar. 1995. *A Mayan Life.* Trans. Elaine Elliot. Rancho Palo Verdes, Cal.: Yax Te' Press.

Graham, Ian, ed. 1975. *Corpus of Maya Hieroglyphic Inscriptions.* Vol.1 (Introduction). Cambridge, Mass.: Peabody Museum of Archaeology and Ethnology, Harvard University.

Green, Duncan. 1992. *Guatemala: Burden of Paradise*. London: Latin America Bureau.

Green, Linda. 1994. "Fear as a Way of Life," *Cultural Anthropology*, 9(2): 227-56.

Guatemalan Church in Exile. 1988. *Guatemala: Security, Development, and Democracy*. Mexico City: Guatemalan Church in Exile.

Handy, Jim. 1984. *Gift of the Devil: A History of Guatemala*. Toronto: Between the Lines.

Handy, Jim. 1994. *Revolution in the Countryside: Rural Conflict and Agrarian Reform in Guatemala, 1944-1954*. Chapel Hill and London: University of North Carolina Press.

Hay, Clarence L., Ralph L. Linton, Samuel K. Lothrop, Harry L. Shapiro, and George C. Vaillant, eds. 1940. *The Maya and Their Neighbors*. New York: D. Appleton Century.

Hill, Robert M. II. 1991. *Colonial Cakchiquels: Highland Maya Adaptations to Spanish Rule, 1600-1700*. Fort Worth, Tx.: Harcourt, Brace, Jovanovich.

Hooks, Margaret, ed. 1993. *Guatemalan Women Speak*. Washington, D.C.: Ecumenical Program on Central America and the Caribbean.

Houston, Stephen D. 1989. *Maya Glyphs*. London: British Museum.

Huxley, Aldous. 1934. *Beyond the Mexique Bay*. London: Chatto and Windus.

Immerman, Richard. 1982. *The CIA in Guatemala: The Foreign Policy of Intervention*. Austin: University of Texas Press.

Jonas, Susanne. 1991. *The Battle for Guatemala: Rebels, Death Squads, and U.S. Power*. Boulder, Col.: Westview Press.

Jones, Grant D. 1989. *Maya Resistance to Spanish Rule: Time and History on a Colonial Frontier*. Albuquerque: University of New Mexico Press.

Kendall, Carl, John Hawkins, and Laurel Bossen, eds. 1983. *Heritage of Conquest: Thirty Years Later*. Albuquerque: University of New Mexico Press.

Kelley, David H. 1976. *Deciphering the Maya Script*. Austin: University of Texas Press.

Kramer, Wendy. 1994. *Encomienda Politics in Early Colonial Guatemala, 1524-*

*1544: Dividing the Spoils*. Boulder, San Francisco, and Oxford: Westview Press.

La Farge, Oliver. 1940. "Maya Ethnology: The Sequence of Cultures," in *The Maya and Their Neighbours*, ed. C.L. Hay et al. New York: D. Appleton Century.

La Farge, Oliver. 1947. *Santa Eulalia: The Religion of a Cuchumatán Indian Town*. Chicago: University of Chicago Press.

La Farge, Oliver and Douglas Byers. 1931. *The Year Bearer's People*. New Orleans: Tulane University Press.

León-Portilla, Miguel. 1988. *Time and Reality in the Thought of the Maya*. 2nd ed. Norman and London: University of Oklahoma Press.

Levenson-Estrada, Deborah. 1994. *Trade Unionists against Terror: Guatemala City, 1954-85*. Chapel Hill and London: University of North Carolina Press.

Lincoln, Jackson S. 1945. *An Ethnographic Study of the Ixil Indians of the Guatemalan Highlands*. Chicago: Microfilm Collection of Manuscripts on Middle American Cultural Anthropology, University of Chicago.

Lovell, W. George. 1992. *Conquest and Survival in Colonial Guatemala: A Historical Geography of the Cuchumatán Highlands, 1500-1821*. Rev. ed. Montreal and Kingston, Ont.: McGill-Queen's University Press.

Lovell, W. George and Christopher H. Lutz. 1995. *Demography and Empire: A Guide to the Population History of Spanish Central America, 1500-1821*. Boulder, Col., San Francisco, and Oxford: Westview Press.

Lovell, W. George and William R. Swezey. 1990. "Indian Migration and Community Formation: An Analysis of *Congregación* in Colonial Guatemala," in *Migration in Colonial Spanish America*, ed. David J. Robinson. Cambridge: Cambridge University Press.

Lutz, Christopher H. 1994. *Santiago de Guatemala, 1541-1773: City, Caste, and the Colonial Experience*. Norman and London: University of Oklahoma Press.

Mackie, Sedley J., ed. [1924] 1978. *An Account of the Conquest of Guatemala in 1524 by Pedro de Alvarado*. Boston: Longwood Press.

MacLeod, Murdo J. 1973. *Spanish Central America: A Socioeconomic History, 1520-1720*. Berkeley, Los Angeles, and London: University of California Press.

Manz, Beatriz. 1988. *Refugees of a Hidden War: The Aftermath of Counterinsurgency in Guatemala*. Albany: State University of New York Press.

Markman, Sidney D. 1966. *Colonial Architecture of Antigua Guatemala*. Philadelphia: American Philosophical Society.

Maudslay, Anne C. and Alfred P. Maudslay. [1899] 1979. *A Glimpse at Guatemala and Some Notes on the Ancient Monuments of Central America*. New York: Blaine Ethridge.

Mayers, Marvin K., ed. 1966. *Languages of Guatemala*. The Hague: Mouton and Company.

McCreery, David. 1988. "Land, Labor, and Violence in Highland Guatemala: San Juan Ixcoy (Huehuetenango), 1890-1940," *The Americas*, 45(2): 237-49.

McCreery, David. 1990. "State Power, Indigenous Communities, and Land in Nineteenth-Century Guatemala, 1820-1920," in *Guatemalan Indians and the State: 1540 to 1988*, ed. Carol A. Smith. Austin: University of Texas Press.

McCreery, David. 1994. *Rural Guatemala, 1760-1940*. Stanford, Cal.: Stanford University Press.

Menchú, Rigoberta. 1984. *I, Rigoberta Menchú: An Indian Woman in Guatemala*. Ed. Elisabeth Burgos-Debray, trans. Ann Wright. London: Verso.

Montejo, Victor. 1984. *El Kanil: Man of Lightning*. Trans. Wallace Kaufman. Carrboro, N.C.: Signal Books.

Montejo, Victor. 1987. *Testimony: Death of a Guatemalan Village*. Trans. Victor Perera. Willimantic, Conn.: Curbstone Press.

Montejo, Victor. 1991. *The Bird Who Cleans the World and Other Mayan Fables*. Trans. Wallace Kaufman. Willimantic, Conn.: Curbstone Press.

Morley, Sylvanus G. [1915] 1975. *An Introduction to the Study of the Maya Hieroglyphs*. New York: Dover Publications.

Naylor, Robert A. 1967. "Guatemala: Indian Attitudes toward Land Tenure," *Journal of Inter-American Studies*, 9(4): 619-39.

Newton, A.P., ed. 1928. *The English-American: A New Survey of the West Indies*. London: George Routledge and Sons.

Oakes, Maud. 1951a. *Beyond the Windy Place: Life in the Guatemalan Highlands*. New York: Farrar, Straus, and Young.

Oakes, Maud. 1951b. *The Two Crosses of Todos Santos: Survivals of Mayan Religious Ritual*. Princeton, N.J.: Princeton University Press.

Painter, James. 1987. *Guatemala: False Hope, False Freedom*. London: Catholic Institute for International Relations and Latin America Bureau.

Orellana, Sandra L. 1984. *The Tzutujil Mayas: Continuity and Change, 1250-1630*. Norman: University of Oklahoma Press.

Payeras, Mario. 1983. *Days of the Jungle: The Testimony of a Guatemalan Guerrillero, 1972-1976*. Trans. George Black. New York: Monthly Review Press.

Perera, Victor. 1993. *Unfinished Conquest: The Guatemalan Tragedy*. Berkeley, Los Angeles, and London: University of California Press.

Proskouriakoff, Tatiana. 1960. "Historical Implications of a Pattern of Dates at Piedras Negras," *American Antiquity*, 25: 454-75.

Recinos, Adrián, trans. 1950. *Popol Vuh: The Sacred Book of the Ancient Quiché Maya*. Norman: University of Oklahoma Press.

Recinos, Adrián and Delia Goetz, trans. 1953. *The Annals of the Cakchiquels*. Norman: University of Oklahoma Press.

Schele, Linda and David Freidel. 1990. *A Forest of Kings: The Untold Story of the Ancient Maya*. New York: William Morrow.

Schele, Linda and Mary E. Miller. 1986. *The Blood of Kings*. New York: George Braziller.

Schevill, Margot Blum. 1993. *Maya Textiles of Guatemala*. Austin: University of Texas Press.

Schirmer, Jennifer. 1995. *A Violence Called Democracy: The Guatemalan Military Project, 1982-1992*. Philadelphia: University of Pennsylvania Press.

Schlesinger, Stephen and Stephen Kinzer. 1982. *Bitter Fruit: The Untold Story of the American Coup in Guatemala*. Garden City, N.Y.: Doubleday.

Sexton, James D., ed. and trans. 1981. *Son of Tecún Umán: A Maya Indian Tells His Life Story*. Tucson: University of Arizona Press.

Sexton, James D., ed. and trans. 1985. *Campesino: The Diary of a Guatemalan Indian*. Tucson: University of Arizona Press.

Sexton, James D., ed. and trans. 1992a. *Ignacio: The Diary of a Maya Indian of Guatemala*. Philadelphia: University of Pennsylvania Press.

Sexton, James D., ed. and trans. 1992b. *Mayan Folktales: Folklore from Lake Atitlán*. New York: Doubleday.

Sherman, William L. 1979. *Forced Native Labor in Sixteenth-Century Central America.* Lincoln and London: University of Nebraska Press.

Simon, Jean-Marie. 1987. *Guatemala: Eternal Spring, Eternal Tyranny.* New York: W.W. Norton.

Smith, Carol A. 1984. "Local History in Global Context: Social and Economic Transitions in Western Guatemala," *Comparative Studies in Society and History*, 26(2): 193-228.

Smith, Carol A., ed. 1990. *Guatemalan Indians and the State: 1540 to 1988.* Austin: University of Texas Press.

Smith, Carol A. 1991. "Maya Nationalism," *NACLA Report on the Americas*, 25(3): 28-33.

Smith-Ayala, Emilie. 1991. *The Granddaughters of Ixmucané: Guatemalan Women Speak.* Toronto: The Women's Press.

Stephens, John L. [1841] 1969. *Incidents of Travel in Central America, Chiapas, and Yucatán.* 2 vols. New York: Dover Publications.

Stoll, David. 1993. *Between Two Armies in the Ixil Towns of Guatemala.* New York: Columbia University Press.

Sullivan, Paul. 1989. *Unfinished Conversations: Mayas and Foreigners between Two Wars.* New York: Alfred A. Knopf.

Taussig, Michael. 1984. "Culture of Terror, Space of Death: Roger Casement's Putomayo Report and the Explanation of Torture," *Comparative Studies in Society and History*, 26(3): 467-97.

Taussig, Michael. 1987. *Shamanism, Colonialism, and the Wild Man: A Study in Terror and Healing.* Chicago: University of Chicago Press.

Tax, Sol, ed. 1950. *Heritage of Conquest: The Ethnology of Middle America.* New York: Macmillan.

Tedlock, Barbara. 1992. *Time and the Highland Maya.* Rev. ed. Albuquerque: University of New Mexico Press.

Tedlock, Dennis, trans. 1985. *Popol Vuh: The Mayan Book of the Dawn of Life.* New York: Simon and Schuster.

Tedlock, Dennis. 1993. "Torture in the Archives: Mayans Meet Europeans," *American Anthropologist*, 95(1): 139-52.

Thompson, J. Eric S., ed. 1958. *Thomas Gage's Travels in the New World*. Norman: University of Oklahoma Press.

Thompson, J. Eric S. 1960. *Maya Hieroglyphic Writing: An Introduction*. Norman: University of Oklahoma Press.

Trudeau, Robert H. 1993. *Guatemalan Politics: The Popular Struggle for Democracy*. Boulder, Col., and London: Lynne Rienner Publishers.

Van Oss, Adriaan C. 1986. *Catholic Colonialism: A Parish History of Guatemala*. Cambridge: Cambridge University Press.

Vigil, Ralph H. 1987. *Alonso de Zorita: Royal Judge and Christian Humanist, 1512-1585*. Norman and London: University of Oklahoma Press.

Vlach, Norita. 1992. *The Quetzal in Flight: Guatemalan Refugee Families in the United States*. Westport, Conn.: Praeger Publishers.

Wagley, Charles. 1941. *Economics of a Guatemalan Village*. Menasha, Wis.: American Anthropological Association.

Wagley, Charles. 1949. *The Social and Religious Life of a Guatemalan Village*. Menasha, Wis.: American Anthropological Association.

Warren, Kay B. 1992. "Transforming Memories and Histories: The Meaning of Ethnic Resurgence for Mayan Indians," in *Americas: New Interpretive Essays*, ed. Alfred Stepan. New York: Oxford University Press.

Warren, Kay B. 1994. "Language and the Politics of Self-Expression: Mayan Revitalization in Guatemala," *Cultural Survival Quarterly*, 18(2,3): 81-86.

Wasserstrom, Robert. 1975. "Revolution in Guatemala: Peasants and Politics under the Arbenz Government," *Comparative Studies in Society and History*, 17(4): 443-78.

Watanabe, John M. 1990. "Enduring Yet Ineffable Community in the Western Periphery of Guatemala," in *Guatemalan Indians and the State: 1540 to 1988*, ed. Carol A. Smith. Austin: University of Texas Press.

Watanabe, John M. 1992. *Maya Saints and Souls in a Changing World*. Austin: University of Texas Press.

Watanabe, John M. 1995. "Unimagining the Maya: Anthropologists, Others, and the Inescapable Hubris of Authorship," *Bulletin of Latin American Research*, 14(1): 25-45.

Williams, Robert G. 1994. *States and Social Evolution: Coffee and the Rise of National Governments in Central America.* Chapel Hill and London: University of North Carolina Press.

Wilson, Richard. 1991. "Machine Guns and Mountain Spirits: The Cultural Effects of State Repression among the Q'eqchi' of Guatemala," *Critique of Anthropology*, 11(1): 33-61.

Wilson, Richard. 1993. "Anchored Communities: Identity and History of the Maya-Q'eqchi'," *Man*, 28(1): 121-38.

Wilson, Richard. 1995. *Maya Resurgence in Guatemala: Q'eqchi' Experiences.* Norman and London: University of Oklahoma Press.

Woodward, Ralph Lee, Jr. 1990. "Changes in the Nineteenth-Century Guatemalan State and Its Indian Policies," in *Guatemalan Indians and the State: 1540 to 1988*, ed. Carol A. Smith. Austin: University of Texas Press.

Woodward, Ralph Lee, Jr. 1993. *Rafael Carrera and the Emergence of the Republic of Guatemala, 1821-1871.* Athens and London: University of Georgia Press.

Wortman, Miles L. 1982. *Government and Society in Central America, 1680-1840.* New York: Columbia University Press.

Wright, Ronald. 1989. *Time among the Maya: Travels in Belize, Guatemala, and Mexico.* Markham, Ont.: Penguin Books.

Wright, Ronald. 1992. *Stolen Continents: The Americas through Indian Eyes Since 1492.* Boston: Houghton Mifflin Company.